Year 4
Practice Book 4A

White Rose Maths Edition

What did you do in maths in Year 3?

Draw or write what you enjoyed doing most.

This book belongs to _____ .

My class is _____ .

Series editor: Tony Staneff

Lead author: Josh Lury

Consultants (first edition): Professor Liu Jian and Professor Zhang Dan

Author team (first edition): Tony Staneff, Josh Lury, Neil Jarrett, Stephen Monaghan, Beth Smith and Paul Wrangles

Contents

This looks like a good challenge!

It is time to start!

How to use this book

Do you remember how to use this **Practice Book**?

Use the **Textbook** first to learn how to solve this type of problem.

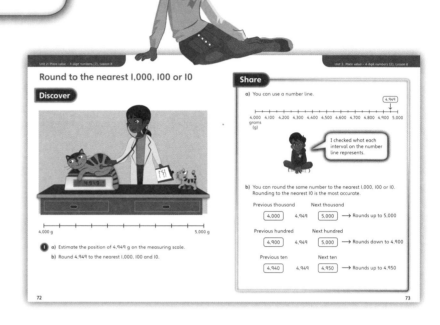

This shows you which **Textbook** page you need.

Have a go at questions by yourself using this **Practice Book**. Use what you have learnt.

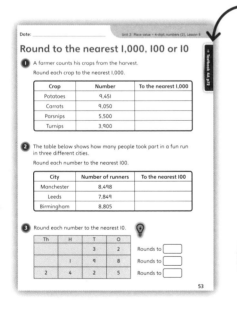

Challenge questions make you think hard!

Questions with this light bulb make you think differently.

Reflect

Each lesson ends with a Reflect question so you can think about what you have learnt.

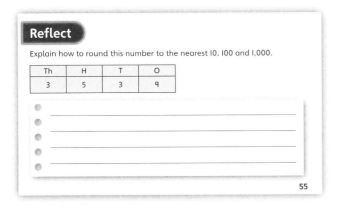

Use My Power Points at the back of this book to keep track of what you have learnt.

My journal

At the end of a unit your teacher will ask you to fill in My journal.

This will help you show how much you can do now that you have finished the unit.

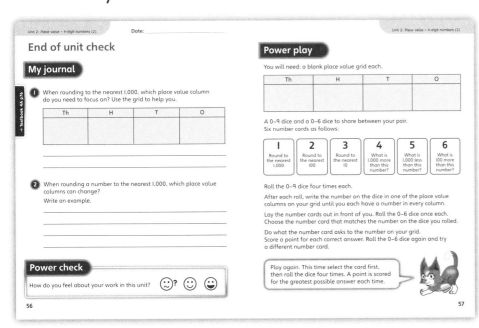

Date: _____

Represent and partition numbers to 1,000

1 Write each number.

a)
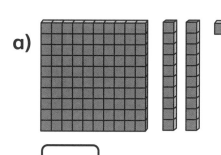

c)

b)
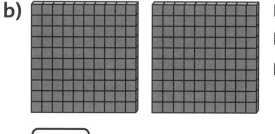

d)
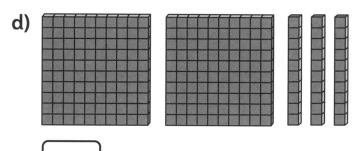

2 Draw or make each number.

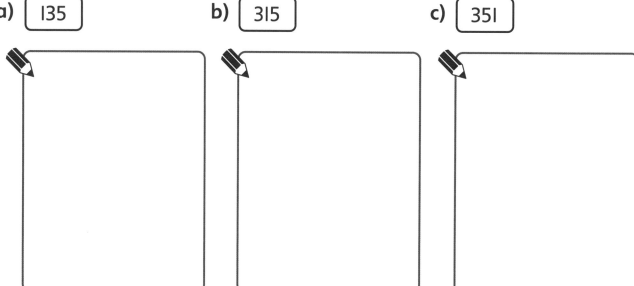

a) 135

b) 315

c) 351

3 Circle the correct value of each underlined digit.

    a) 3<u>2</u>5   [2 hundreds]   [2 tens]   [2 ones]

    b) <u>2</u>05   [2 hundreds]   [2 tens]   [2 ones]

    c) 20<u>2</u>   [2 hundreds]   [2 tens]   [2 ones]

4 Partition the numbers.

    a) 892 = ☐ hundreds ☐ tens and ☐ ones

    b) 705 = ☐ hundreds ☐ tens and ☐ ones

5 Complete the part-whole models and number sentences.

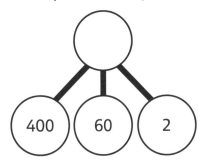
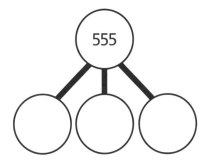

☐ = 400 + 60 + 2   555 = ☐ + ☐ + ☐

6 Complete the additions.

    a) ☐ = 400 + 50 + 2   **f)** ☐ = 90 + 700

    b) ☐ = 3 + 70 + 900   **g)** 864 = 800 + ☐ + 4

    c) ☐ = 300 + 20   **h)** 936 = 6 + 30 + ☐

    d) ☐ = 800 + 7   **i)** 573 = 500 + 3 + ☐

    e) ☐ = 3 + 600   **j)** 771 = 70 + 1 + ☐

CHALLENGE

7 You can make 212 using 5 counters.

H	T	O
⊙⊙	⊙	⊙⊙

a) List all the numbers you can make using exactly 5 counters.

_____

_____

_____

_____

_____

b) Can you be sure you have found them all?
Investigate the same puzzle using 6 counters.

Reflect

List all the 3-digit numbers that have 6 ones and 2 hundreds.

_____

_____

_____

_____

_____

_____

Number line to 1,000

1 Write the missing numbers.

a)

0 ☐ ☐ ☐ ☐ ☐ ☐ ☐ ☐ ☐ 1,000

b)

600 ☐ ☐ ☐ ☐ ☐ ☐ ☐ ☐ ☐ 700

c)

650 ☐ ☐ ☐ ☐ ☐ ☐ ☐ ☐ ☐ 660

2 Join each number to the correct place.

a)

520   560   530   590   580

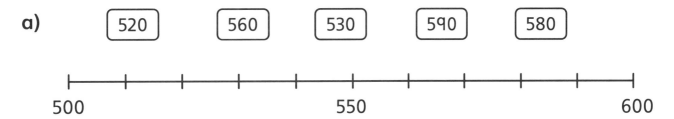

500   550   600

b)

230   210   240   270   280

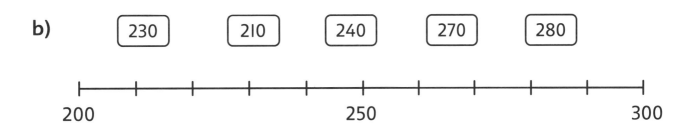

200   250   300

3 Write the numbers shown.

a)

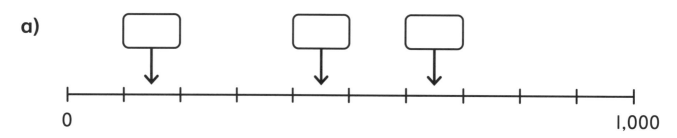

b)

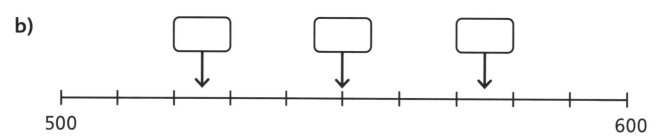

4 Estimate how much is in each jug.

a) [   ] ml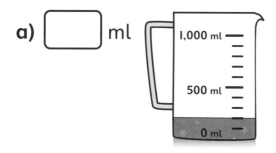

c) [   ] ml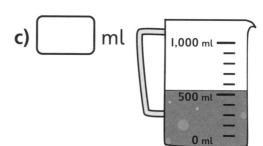

b) [   ] ml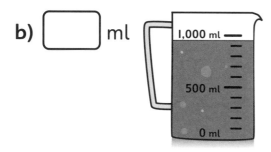

d) [   ] ml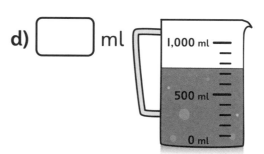

5 Estimate the position of each number on the number line.

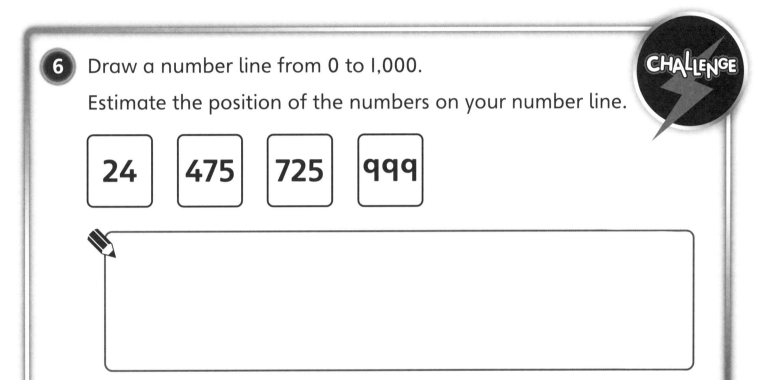

6 Draw a number line from 0 to 1,000.

Estimate the position of the numbers on your number line.

CHALLENGE

24   475   725   999

Reflect

What number is in the middle of a number line?

Date: _____

Multiples of 1,000

1 **a)** Count the cups.

There are ⬚ cups.

b) Count the cups.

There are ⬚ cups.

2 Write these multiples of 1,000.

a)

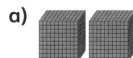

⬚

d)

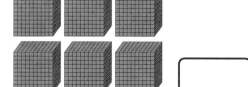

⬚

b)

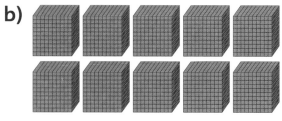

⬚

e)

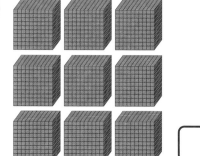

⬚

c)

⬚

3 Complete the number tracks.

a)

2,000	3,000			6,000		8,000

b)

10,000	9,000			6,000		4,000

12

4 Find all the multiples of 1,000.

6	0	1	7	0	4	0	6	0	0	5	7	0	0	0	5
4	0	0	7	0	0	4	0	0	1	5	6	0	8	0	0
0	2	0	7	3	0	4	0	3	0	0	7	4	0	6	4
0	5	8	2	2	8	9	0	0	5	4	0	0	1	4	0
8	0	1	0	0	3	4	5	0	8	3	8	2	7	0	6
0	0	4	0	6	0	8	5	4	5	0	1	0	3	0	0
1	9	7	8	9	3	0	1	5	0	0	2	4	0	0	5
1	0	3	0	0	9	0	5	0	0	0	4	2	3	6	0
0	3	0	5	4	1	0	2	8	4	7	9	0	0	8	6
0	9	5	0	0	5	6	0	0	7	0	1	0	0	0	0

5 2,000 of these pencils are red and 5,000 are blue. The rest are green.

Show how you can work out how many green pencils there are.

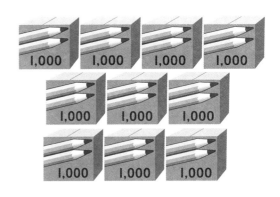

1,000 1,000 1,000 1,000
1,000 1,000 1,000
1,000 1,000 1,000

6 Circle the correct answers.

CHALLENGE

a) I thousand is equal to:

    10 ones   10 tens   10 hundreds   100 hundreds

b) 3 thousands is equal to:

    30 tens   30 hundreds   300 ones   3, 000 ones

c) 50 hundreds is equal to:

    5 tens   50 hundreds   5 thousands   500 ones

d) 700 tens is equal to:

    70 ones   7 hundreds   7 thousands   700 ones

Reflect

Play a 'Count in 1,000s' game with a partner.

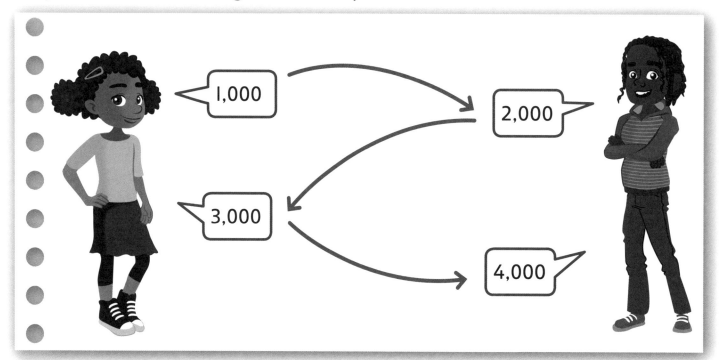

4-digit numbers

↓ Textbook 4A p20

1 Match the pairs.

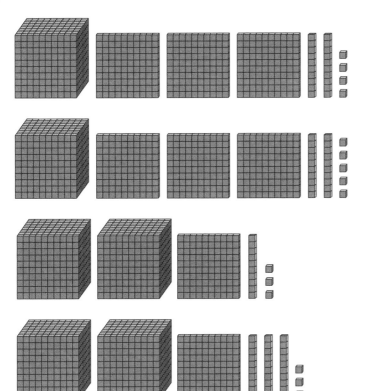

1,325

2,133

1,324

2,113

2 Write each number.

a)

Th	H	T	O
1,000 1,000	100 100	10 10 10	1

b)

Th	H	T	O
1,000 1,000	100 100 100	10 10	1 1

c)

Th	H	T	O
1,000 1,000 1,000 1,000	100 100 100	10 10 10 10	

d)

Th	H	T	O
1,000 1,000	100		1 1 1 1

15

3 Draw place value counters to show each number.

(I) (10) (100) (1,000)

a)
2,223

b)
2,121

c)
2,021

d)
2,020

4 Use each card once.

Make as many different 4-digit numbers as you can.

q   q

8   8

_____

_____

_____

_____

_____

5 Here is a mystery 4-digit number.

Each symbol represents a different 1-digit number.

 $\times$ ◆ = 30

 ◆ – ▲ = 1

 ◆ – ● – ♥ = ▲

 ◆ – ♥ = 6

What is the mystery 4-digit number? ▢

Reflect

5 6 ✳ 5

What could this number be?

_____

_____

_____

_____

_____

Date: _____

Partition 4-digit numbers

1 a) Partition each number into thousands, hundreds, tens and ones.

2,324 = ⬜ thousands, ⬜ hundreds, ⬜ tens and ⬜ ones

6,281 = ⬜ thousands, ⬜ hundreds, ⬜ tens and ⬜ ones

4,427 = ⬜ thousands, ⬜ hundreds, ⬜ tens and ⬜ ones

9,988 = ⬜ thousands, ⬜ hundreds, ⬜ tens and ⬜ ones

b) Complete each number

⬜ = 5 thousands, 2 hundreds, 3 tens and 7 ones

⬜ = 2 thousands, 8 hundreds, 9 tens and 4 ones

⬜ = 9 thousands, 1 hundred, 3 tens and 6 ones

⬜ = 7 thousands, 6 hundreds, 5 tens and 4 ones

2 Complete each partition as an addition.

a) ⬜ = 3,000 + 500 + 10 + 1

b) ⬜ = 5,000 + 300 + 90 + 3

c) ⬜ = 5 + 30 + 900 + 7,000

d) ⬜ = 9,000 + 7 + 50 + 300

e) 1,574 = 4 + 70 + ⬜ + 1,000

f) 4,141 = 1 + 40 + 100 + ⬜

3 Use a tick to show the value of each underlined digit.

	5	50	500	5,000
2,552				
5,235				
1,555				
5,055				

4 Join matching pairs.

2,068		2,000 + 800 + 6
2,608		6,000 + 800 + 2
2,806		2,000 + 60 + 8
2,680		2,000 + 600 + 80
6,820		6,000 + 800 + 20
6,802		2,000 + 600 + 8

5 Partition each number into place value additions.

a) 4,400 = _____

b) 4,040 = _____

c) 4,004 = _____

d) 3,030 = _____

e) 1,010 = _____

f) 6,060 = _____

6 Andy has made a number. He says:

CHALLENGE

- My number has the same number of 1,000s and 10s.
- There are two more 1s than 10s.
- The 100s digit is half the 1,000s digit.

What could Andy's number be?

Draw place value counters to show the possible answers.

Reflect

Make up your own mystery number puzzle.

Challenge a partner to solve it.

Partition 4-digit numbers flexibly

→ Textbook 4A p28

1 Find five different ways to partition 2,321.

$2,321 = 2,000 + 300 + 20 + 1$

2 Complete the additions.

a) ☐ $= 8,000 + 535$

b) ☐ $= 5,000 + 700 + 24$

c) ☐ $= 2,000 + 1,000 + 44$

d) ☐ $= 1,000 + 1,000 + 600 + 21$

e) ☐ $= 5,000 + 2,300 + 90 + 9$

f) $4,286 = 4,000 + 200 +$ ☐

g) $9,147 = 9,000 +$ ☐

h) $7,565 = 7,500 +$ ☐

i) $5,535 = 5,000 + 500 + 20 +$ ☐

j) $6,177 = 6,000 + 170 +$ ☐

3 Mr Jones has saved £3,000 for a new car.

The car costs £3,750.

How much more does he need to save?

Circle the correct answer.

| £ 75 | £ 1,075 | £ 750 | £ 6,750 |

4 Complete the part-whole model and subtractions.

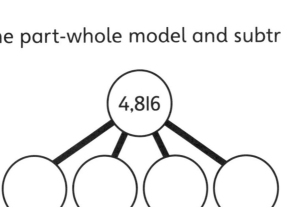

4,816 – 10 = ☐   4,816 – 4,000 = ☐

4,816 – ☐ = 4,016   4,816 – ☐ = 4,810

5 Complete the subtractions.

a) 6,177 – 100 = ☐   b) 4,800 + ☐ = 4,950

c) 5,834 – 30 = ☐   d) 2,440 + ☐ = 2,451

e) 3,054 – ☐ = 3,000   f) ☐ + 725 = 1,825

g) 4,275 – ☐ = 4,005   h) ☐ + 6,005 = 7,505

6 Harry has partitioned a number.

2,000 + 1,700 + 50 + 2

Esma has partitioned the same number in a different way.

3,000 + 600 + [ ]

a) Complete Esma's partition. What is the missing number?

b) Find three more ways to partition Harry's number.

CHALLENGE

_____

_____

_____

_____

Reflect

Show two different ways of partitioning 3,750.

Compare your results with the rest of the class.

Did anyone find the same way as you?

_____

_____

_____

_____

Date: _____

1, 10, 100, 1,000 more or less

1 Use the place value grid to complete the sentences.

a)

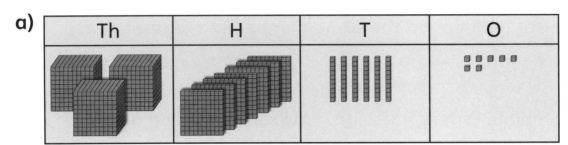

Th	H	T	O

1,000 more than 3,767 is [＿＿＿].

b)

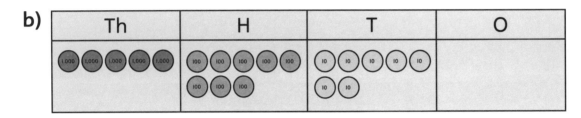

Th	H	T	O

100 more than 5,870 is [＿＿＿].

c)

Th	H	T	O

10 less than [＿＿＿] is [＿＿＿].

d)

Th	H	T	O

1,000 less than [＿＿＿] is [＿＿＿].

2 Write the number shown by each representation, then complete the table.

Number	Number in digits	1,000 more	100 less	10 more
(1,000 ×4, 100 ×4, 1 ×7)				
(base ten blocks and number line 0 to 3,000)				
Seven hundred and fifty-eight				

3 Fill in the missing numbers to make the sentences correct.

a) 1,000 more than 4,879 is ⬚.

b) 100 less than 4,879 is ⬚.

c) 10 more than ⬚ is 4,879.

d) 1 more than 4,879 is ⬚.

e) 3,921 is 1,000 more than ⬚.

f) 100 less than ⬚ is 652.

25

4 Complete each number sentence.

a) ⬚ more than 2,875 is 2,876.

b) 5,783 + ⬚ = 6,783

c) ⬚ less than 3,580 is 3,480.

d) ⬚ – 10 = 3,990

e) 5,999 + 1,000 – 10 = ⬚

f) ⬚ + 10 – 100 = 7,860

g) 7,500 is ⬚ less than 8,500.

5 If 6,865 is the output of the function machine, what was the input?

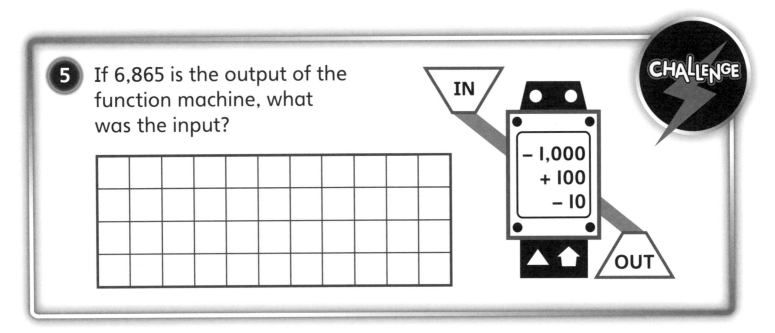

CHALLENGE

IN

– 1,000
+ 100
– 10

OUT

Reflect

When finding 1,000 more or 1,000 less than a 4-digit number, which digits change? How many digits change?

_____

_____

_____

Date: _____

1,000s, 100s, 10s and 1s

 Write each number.

a)

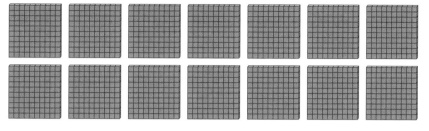

b)

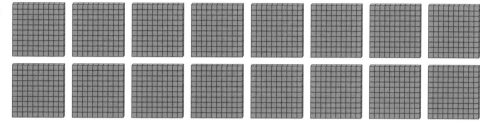

c)

d)

e)

2 Complete each sentence.

a) 37 hundreds is ☐ .

b) 38 hundreds is ☐ .

c) 39 hundreds is ☐ .

d) ☐ hundreds is 4,000.

3 What is the total mass of these weights?

☐ g

4 One length of a swimming pool measures 10 m.

Complete the sentences below.

10 m

a) ☐ lengths measure 100 m.

e) ☐ lengths measure 1,500 m.

b) ☐ lengths measure 500 m.

f) ☐ lengths measure 1,600 m.

c) ☐ lengths measure 1,000 m.

g) ☐ lengths measure 2,000 m.

d) ☐ lengths measure 1,100 m.

h) ☐ lengths measure 1,750 m.

5 Adam represented a number but then knocked over his counters.

What number did he represent?

CHALLENGE

Adam's number was [   ].

Reflect

Explain why 20 hundreds is 2,000.

Date: _____

End of unit check

My journal

↑ Textbook 4A p40

1. Describe the number using as many keywords as you can.

   Represent and draw the number in different ways.

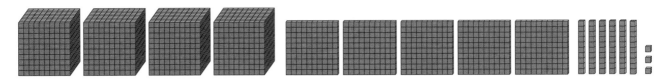

> **Keywords**
>
> 1,000s, 100s, 10s, Is, number line, numerals

_____

_____

_____

Power check

How do you feel about your work in this unit?

Power play

You will need: a place value grid and six blank counters.

Place all six counters on the place value grid to make a number.

Make sure you place at least one counter in each column.

Th	H	T	O

List all the different numbers you can make.

_____

_____

_____

_____

_____

_____

_____

I wonder how my answers will change if I use seven counters.

Date: _____

Number line to 10,000

1 What number does the arrow point to in each number line?

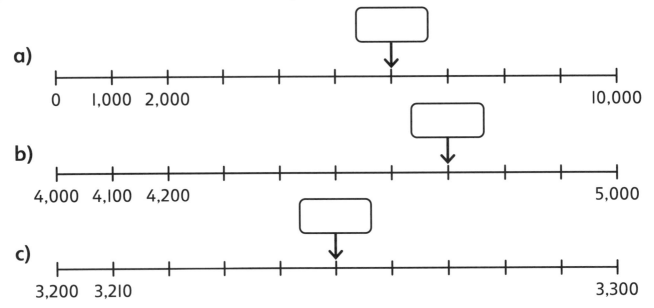

a)
0   1,000   2,000   10,000

b)
4,000   4,100   4,200   5,000

c)
3,200   3,210   3,300

2 Complete the number lines.

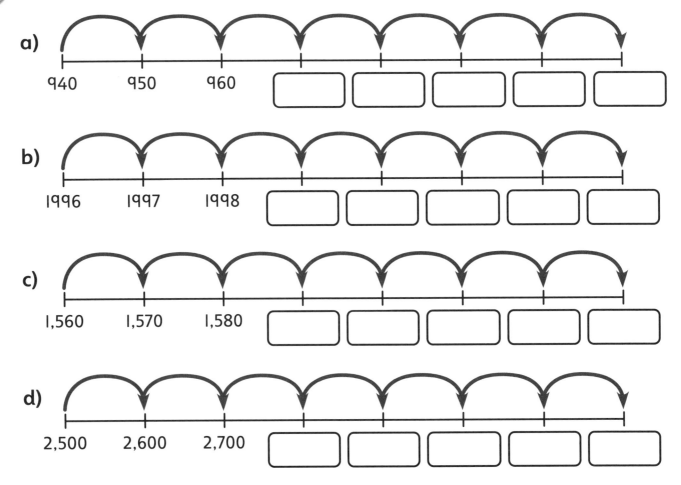

a)
940   950   960

b)
1996   1997   1998

c)
1,560   1,570   1,580

d)
2,500   2,600   2,700

32

3 Write the missing numbers.

a)

b)

c)

4 What is the length of each rope?

a)

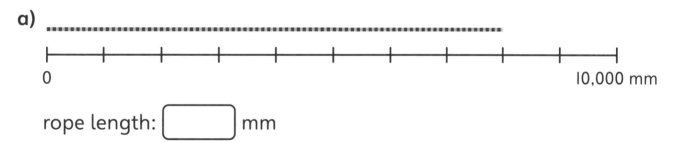

rope length: ⬚ mm

b)

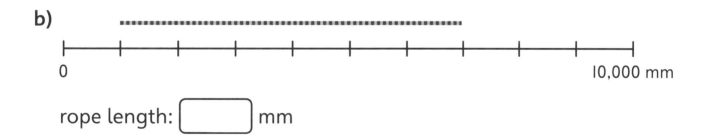

rope length: ⬚ mm

c)

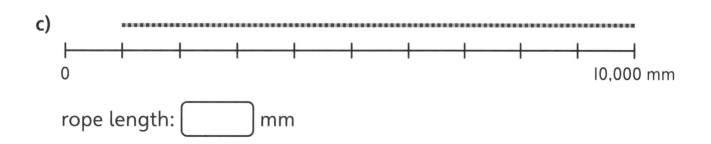

rope length: ⬚ mm

5 Write the missing numbers.

a)
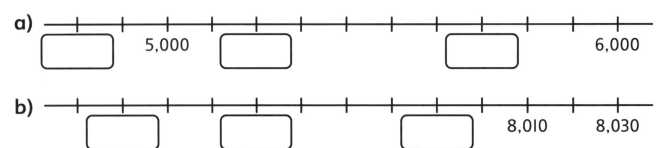

5,000 □ □ 6,000

b)
□ □ □ 8,010 8,030

6 Some more liquid is poured into the jug.

What is the volume of liquid that is added?

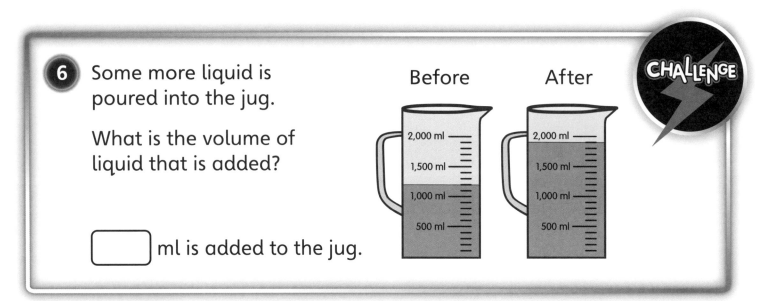

Before   After   CHALLENGE

□ ml is added to the jug.

Reflect

Explain Max's mistake.

9,800 9,801 9,802 9,803 9,804 9,805 9,806 9,807 9,808 9,809 9,900

Max

34

Between two multiples

1 Write three different numbers in each section of the number line.

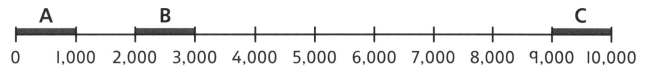

A	B	C

2 Write three different numbers in each section of the number line.

A	B	C

3 Write three different numbers in each section of the number line.

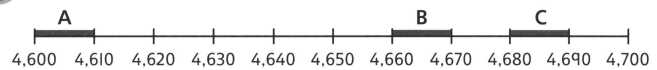

A	B	C

Textbook 4A p48

4 Complete the previous and next multiples.

a) Previous thousand / Next thousand

Previous thousand		Next thousand
☐	4,916	☐
☐	2,837	☐
☐	9,201	☐

d) Previous thousand / Next thousand

Previous thousand		Next thousand
☐	820	☐
☐	5,630	☐
☐	16	☐

b) Previous hundred / Next hundred

Previous hundred		Next hundred
☐	4,916	☐
☐	2,837	☐
☐	9,201	☐

e) Previous hundred / Next hundred

Previous hundred		Next hundred
☐	990	☐
☐	1,040	☐
☐	99	☐

c) Previous ten / Next ten

Previous ten		Next ten
☐	4,916	☐
☐	2,837	☐
☐	9,201	☐

f) Previous ten / Next ten

Previous ten		Next ten
☐	894	☐
☐	9,999	☐
☐	1	☐

5 Use each card once to complete the numbers.

CHALLENGE

| 0 | 0 | 3 | 4 | 9 | 9 |

Previous thousand

4,000

◻,5◻1

Next thousand

5,000

Previous hundred

3,000

◻,◻91

Next hundred

3,100

Previous ten

4,990

4,◻◻7

Next ten

5,000

Reflect

Explain how you find the previous multiple of 1,000 and next multiple of 1,000 for a number.

Date: _____

↑ Textbook 4A p52

Estimate on a number line to 10,000

1 Estimate the numbers shown.

a)

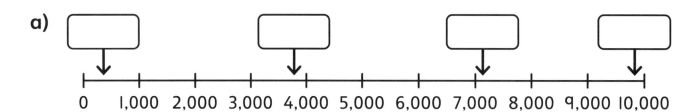

b)

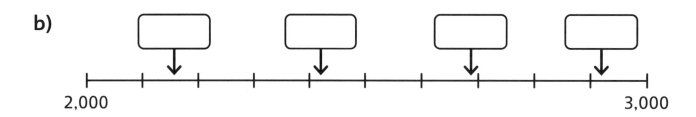

2 Draw lines to estimate the position of each number.

a)

| 3,500 | 4,100 | 4,900 | 7,500 | 7,600 |

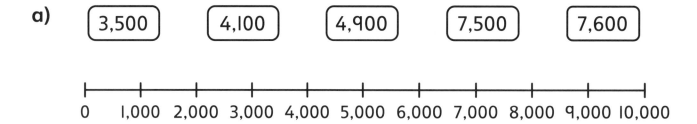

b)

| 1,050 | 1,190 | 1,500 | 1,550 | 1,750 | 1,790 |

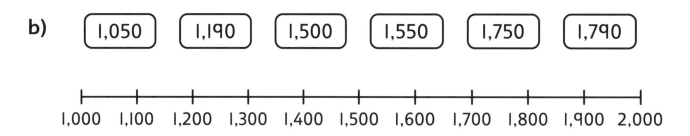

c)

| 6,201 | 6,210 | 6,245 | 6,272 | 6,289 |

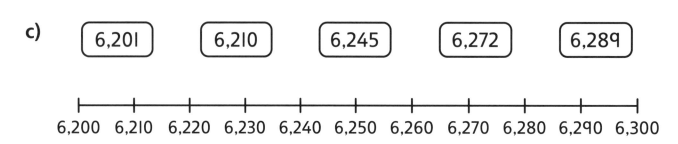

3 Draw water levels for each volume.

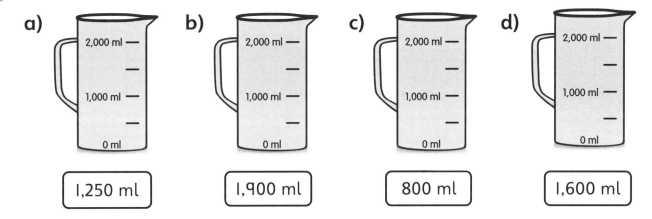

a) 1,250 ml b) 1,900 ml c) 800 ml d) 1,600 ml

4 Estimate the mass shown.

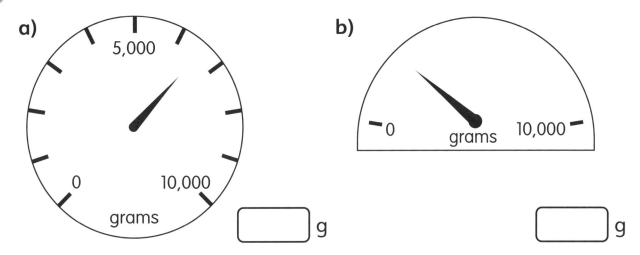

a) [   ] g

b) [   ] g

5 Draw arrows to show the approximate measurement.

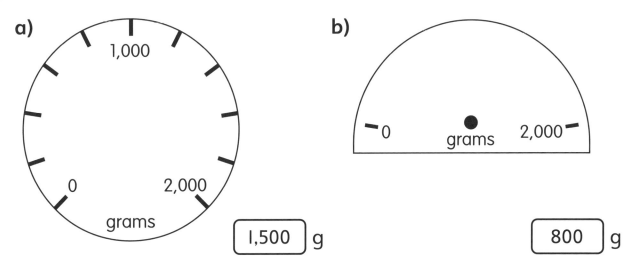

a) 1,500 g

b) 800 g

6 Estimate the length of each ribbon.

CHALLENGE

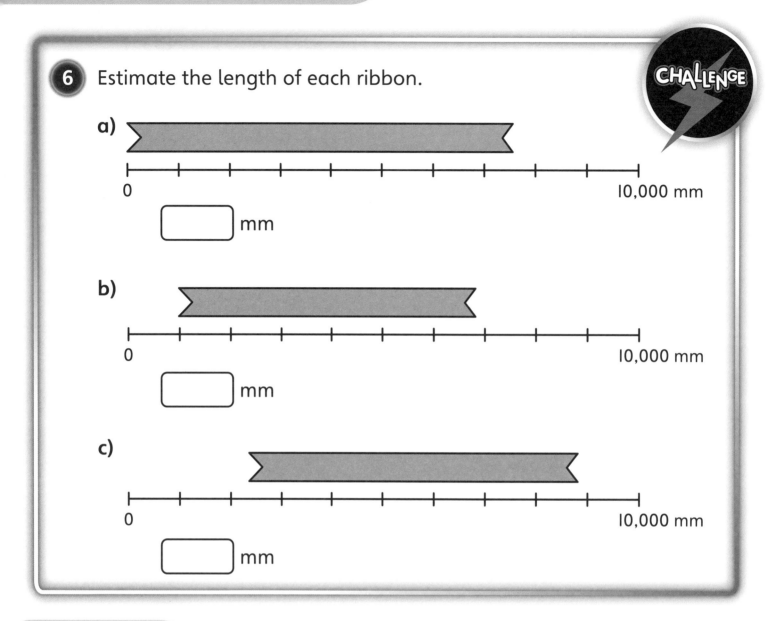

a)

0   10,000 mm

[ ] mm

b)

0   10,000 mm

[ ] mm

c)

0   10,000 mm

[ ] mm

Reflect

Play a game with a partner. Say a 4-digit number. Mark it on the line. Take it in turns. Try to get three of your numbers without any of your partner's numbers in between.

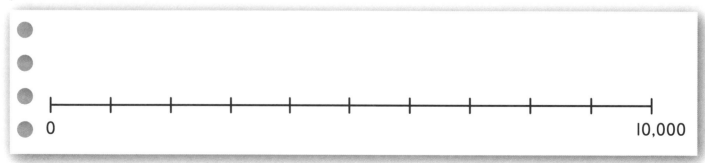

0   10,000

Compare and order numbers to 10,000

① Tick the greater number in each pair.

a)

Th	H	T	O
5	0	1	5
4	3	0	1

b)

Th	H	T	O
6	7	2	3
6	7	5	1

c)

Th	H	T	O
	9	4	5
4	7	8	1

d)

Th	H	T	O
	9	8	0
1	0	0	3

e)

Th	H	T	O
7	6	5	0
9	2	4	8

f)

Th	H	T	O
3	1	6	2
3	0	9	9

② Complete using < or >.

a) 3,560 ◯ 3,650

b) 2,886 ◯ 2,888

c) 2,848 ◯ 2,851

d) 3,560 ◯ 3,660

e) 2,686 ◯ 5,886

f) 2,846 ◯ 2,848

③ Complete the missing digits.

a) 4,☐78 < 4,592

b) 7,8☐9 < 7,8☐4

c) 5,04☐ < ☐,042

I wonder if there is more than one digit that would work in each empty box.

41

Textbook 4A p56

4 Order the numbers from smallest to greatest.

Th	H	T	O
6	5	3	6
6	4	2	1
6	5	4	1

Smallest ⟶ ◯ ⟶ ◯ ⟶ ◯ ⟶ Greatest

5 Order the numbers in descending order.

a) 4,502 kg   3,821 kg   4,314 kg   4,099 kg

◯ ◯ ◯ ◯

b) 812 m   8,032 m   8,120 m   7,830 m   7,909 m

◯ ◯ ◯ ◯ ◯

6 Max, Lexi and Richard track their activities for a month to see how far they swim, run and cycle.

	Swim	Run	Cycle
Max	2,500 m	3,400 m	7,850 m
Lexi	750 m	4,500 m	7,995 m
Richard	2,350 m	4,180 m	7,855 m

a) Who swam the furthest?   ◯

b) Who ran the second shortest distance?   ◯

c) Put the distances they cycled in order, starting with the shortest.

◯ ◯ ◯

7 Zac has put five 4-digit numbers in ascending order.

4,317, ☐ , ☐ , ☐ , 4,353

All the numbers have a digit sum of 15.

What are the other three numbers?

CHALLENGE

A digit sum is the sum of all the digits in a number.

Reflect

Use the digits 5, 6, 8 and 9 to make some 4-digit numbers.

Then write your numbers in desending order.

Date: _____

Round to the nearest 1,000

1 Round each number to the nearest 1,000.

a)

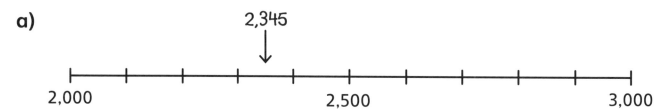

2,345 rounded to the nearest 1,000 is [   ].

b)

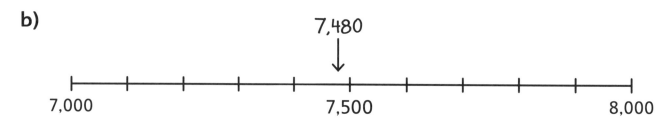

7,480 rounded to the nearest 1,000 is [   ].

c)

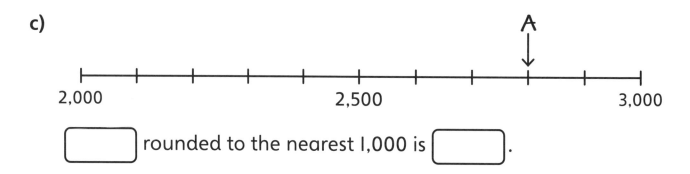

[   ] rounded to the nearest 1,000 is [   ].

2 Is each number closer to the previous or next multiple of 1,000?

Tick your answer.

	Previous thousand		Next thousand
a)	4,000	4,991	5,000
b)	4,000	4,291	5,000
c)	4,000	4,691	5,000

3 Round each number to the nearest 1,000.

Holiday destination	Visitors per day	Nearest 1,000
Paris	8,782	
Sydney	9,259	
Pisa	5,160	
New York	3,500	

4 **a)** On the number line, mark five numbers that round to 1,000 to the nearest 1,000.

0   1,000   2,000

b) On the number line, mark five numbers that round to 5,000 to the nearest 1,000.

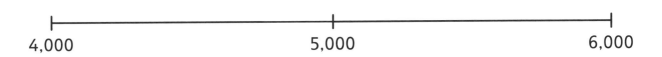

4,000   5,000   6,000

CHALLENGE

5 Isla, Zac and Aki each make a 4-digit number.

When rounded to the nearest 1,000, all of their numbers are 5,000.

What could their numbers be?

	Th	H	T	O
Isla	5	3	☐	5
Zac	4	☐	0	0
Aki	☐	4	9	9

I am going to see if it makes a difference what numbers are put in the boxes.

Reflect

Describe in steps how to round a number to the nearest 1,000.

Round to the nearest 100

1 Round to the nearest 100.

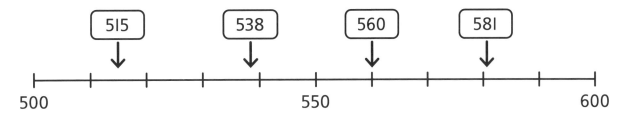

a) 515 rounded to the nearest 100 is ⬜.

b) 538 rounded to the nearest 100 is ⬜.

c) 560 rounded to the nearest 100 is ⬜.

d) 581 rounded to the nearest 100 is ⬜.

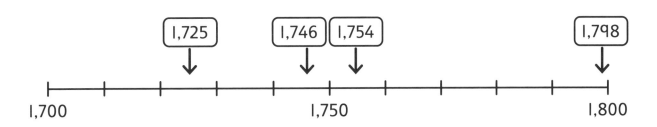

e) 1,725 rounded to the nearest 100 is ⬜.

f) 1,746 rounded to the nearest 100 is ⬜.

g) 1,754 rounded to the nearest 100 is ⬜.

h) 1,798 rounded to the nearest 100 is ⬜.

2 Round each number to the nearest 100.

Previous hundred		Next hundred
a)	320	
b)	350	
c)	1,290	
d)	2,447	
e)	4,005	

3 Round the numbers to the nearest hundred.

a) 768   e) 951

b) 402   f) 12

c) 199   g) 420

d) 84   h) 1,001

4 Bella says 250 can be rounded to either 200 or 300 because it is in the middle of these numbers.

Richard disagrees and says it rounds down to 200.

Do you agree with Bella or Richard? Explain your answer.

_____

_____

_____

_____

5 Max has three digit cards.

He makes a 3-digit number that rounds to 500 to the nearest hundred.

What numbers could Max have made?

_____

_____

_____

| 3 | 4 | 5 |

6 Maria has four digit cards.

| 3 | 4 | 5 | 4 |

CHALLENGE

She makes a number that rounds to 4,500 to the nearest 100 and 4,000 to the nearest thousand.

What number does she make? [   ]

Reflect

Explain why one of these numbers rounds up and one rounds down, to the nearest 100.

| 1,450 | | 2,325 |

_____

_____

_____

_____

Date: _____

Round to the nearest 10

1 Complete the sentences.

132 rounds to ⬚ to the nearest 10.

137 rounds to ⬚ to the nearest 10.

2 Write the previous and next 10 for each number.

	Previous ten		Next ten			Previous ten		Next ten
a)	⬚	57	⬚		c)	⬚	136	⬚
b)	⬚	12	⬚		d)	⬚	502	⬚

3 Round the numbers to the nearest 10.

a) 18 to the nearest 10 is ⬚.

b) 28 to the nearest 10 is ⬚.

c) 81 to the nearest 10 is ⬚.

d) 82 to the nearest 10 is ⬚.

e) 124 to the nearest 10 is ⬚.

f) 126 to the nearest 10 is ⬚.

g) 368 to the nearest 10 is ⬚.

h) 995 to the nearest 10 is ⬚.

4 **a)** Sort the numbers into the table.

| 15 | 41 | 78 | 102 | 209 | 333 | 457 | 765 | 902 | 981 |

Round down to the nearest 10	Round up to the nearest 10

b) Add two 4-digit numbers to each column.

5 Round the numbers to the nearest 10.

a)   76 [ ]   176 [ ]   376 [ ]

b) 1,024 [ ]   1,124 [ ]   1,324 [ ]

c) 1,715 [ ]   2,715 [ ]   3,715 [ ]

d) 1,704 [ ]   5,704 [ ]   8,704 [ ]

6 Sam has three digit cards. He uses two to make each of the following numbers. What numbers does Sam make?

a) [ ][ ] rounds to 80.

b) [ ][ ] rounds to 80.

| 1 | 7 | 8 |

51

7 Use each digit card once to complete these statements.

CHALLENGE

| 3 | 4 | 4 | 4 | 4 | 4 | 5 | 5 | 5 | 5 | 5 |

☐ rounds to 0 to the nearest 10.

☐ rounds to 10 to the nearest 10.

☐☐ rounds to 50 to the nearest 10.

☐☐☐ rounds to 540 to the nearest 10.

☐☐☐☐ rounds to 5,450 to the nearest 10.

Reflect

Max says, 'When you round a number to the nearest 10, only the 10s digit can change.'

Do you agree with Max? Explain your answer.

Round to the nearest 1,000, 100 or 10

↓ Textbook 4A p72

1) A farmer counts his crops from the harvest.

Round each crop to the nearest 1,000.

Crop	Number	To the nearest 1,000
Potatoes	9,451	
Carrots	9,050	
Parsnips	5,500	
Turnips	3,900	

2) The table below shows how many people took part in a fun run in three different cities.

Round each number to the nearest 100.

City	Number of runners	To the nearest 100
Manchester	8,498	
Leeds	7,849	
Birmingham	8,805	

3) Round each number to the nearest 10.

Th	H	T	O
		3	2
	1	9	8
2	4	2	5

Rounds to [   ]

Rounds to [   ]

Rounds to [   ]

4 Round each number to the nearest 10, 100 and 1,000.

	10	100	1,000
8			
988			
1,899			
9,999			

5 What is the smallest possible and greatest possible number that rounds to:

a) 9,000 to the nearest 1,000   Smallest [   ]   Greatest [   ]

b) 1,400 to the nearest 100   Smallest [   ]   Greatest [   ]

c) 820 to the nearest 10   Smallest [   ]   Greatest [   ]

d) 5,500 to the nearest 100   Smallest [   ]   Greatest [   ]
   and 5,450 to the nearest 10

6 Aki's number rounded to the nearest 10, 100 and 1,000 is 2,000.

What could Aki's number be?

Find all possible solutions.

_____

_____

_____

_____

7 Add the missing digits in the number column.

Then round the numbers.

CHALLENGE

Number	Round to the nearest		
	1,000	100	10
8,341			
6,⬜⬜2			6,890
8,⬜7⬜	9,000		
5,⬜5⬜		5,500	
⬜,⬜⬜7		6,100	6,100

Reflect

Explain how to round this number to the nearest 10, 100 and 1,000.

Th	H	T	O
3	5	3	9

_____

_____

_____

_____

Date: _____

End of unit check

My journal

↑ Textbook 4A p76

1. When rounding to the nearest 1,000, which place value column do you need to focus on? Use the grid to help you.

Th	H	T	O

_____

_____

2. When rounding a number to the nearest 1,000, which place value columns can change?

Write an example.

_____

_____

_____

_____

Power check

How do you feel about your work in this unit?

Power play

You will need: a blank place value grid each.

Th	H	T	O

A 0–9 dice and a 0–6 dice to share between your pair.
Six number cards as follows:

1	**2**	**3**	**4**	**5**	**6**
Round to the nearest 1,000	Round to the nearest 100	Round to the nearest 10	What is 1,000 more than this number?	What is 1,000 less than this number?	What is 100 more than this number?

Roll the 0–9 dice four times each.

After each roll, write the number on the dice in one of the place value columns on your grid until you each have a number in every column.

Lay the number cards out in front of you. Roll the 0–6 dice once each. Choose the number card that matches the number on the dice you rolled.

Do what the number card asks to the number on your grid.
Score a point for each correct answer. Roll the 0–6 dice again and try a different number card.

Play again. This time select the card first, then roll the dice four times. A point is scored for the greatest possible answer each time.

Date: _____

Add and subtract Is, I0s, I00s, 1,000s

1) Complete these calculations.

a)

Th	H	T	O
1,000 1,000 1,000 1,000	100	10 10 10	1 1 1 1 1 / 1 1
			1 1

4,137 + 2 = ☐

b)

Th	H	T	O
1,000 1,000 1,000 1,000	100	10 10 10	1 1 1 1 1 / 1 1
		10 10	

4,137 + 20 = ☐

2) Work out the missing numbers.

Th	H	T	O
1,000 1,000 1,000 1,000 1,000	100 100 100 100 100	10 10 10 10 10	1 1 1 1 1 1
1,000	100	10	1

a) 6,666 + 2 = ☐

6,666 + 20 = ☐

2,000 + 6,666 = ☐

b) 6,666 − 200 = ☐

6,666 = ☐ − 200

6,666 − ☐ = 6,664

3 Complete these calculations.

a) 3,154 + 500 = ☐

b) 500 + 4,351 = ☐

c) 9,786 – 4,000 = ☐

d) ☐ = 7,968 – 400

e) ☐ + 1,000 = 2,134

f) ☐ + 4,000 = 4,521

g) 4,014 – 10 = ☐

h) 5,001 – ☐ = 1

4 a) How much does the car cost now?

£7,999
£1,000 off

£ ☐

b) What is the change in price?

Was £8,749
Now £8,249

£ ☐

5 3,333 + 4,000 = 7,333

Explain how to use this fact to solve 7,333 – 3,333 = ☐.

_____

_____

_____

_____

6 **a)** Use these cards once each to complete all the puzzles.

CHALLENGE

| 100 | 200 | 300 | 400 | 500 | 600 | 700 | 800 | 900 |

$3{,}334 + \boxed{} - \boxed{} = 3{,}434$

$3{,}334 - \boxed{} + \boxed{} = 3{,}434$

$3{,}934 - \boxed{} - \boxed{} = 3{,}434$

$3{,}434 - \boxed{} - \boxed{} + \boxed{} = 3{,}434$

b) Find another way to complete them.

_____

_____

_____

Reflect

$5{,}167 + \boxed{} = 9{,}167$

Show how to work out the missing number.

Add two 4-digit numbers

1 Holly has saved £2,321. Toshi has saved £525.

How much have they saved altogether?

Th	H	T	O
	2	3	2	1
+		5	2	5

Think carefully about what is in each column.

They have saved £ ☐ altogether.

2 Complete the additions.

a)

Th	H	T	O
1,000 1,000 1,000	100		1 1 1 1 1
1,000 1,000 1,000	100 100 100 100 100 10		1

	Th	H	T	O
	3	1	0	5
+	3	5	1	1

3,105 + 3,511 = ☐

b)

Th	H	T	O
1,000 1,000 1,000 1,000 1,000 100		10 10 10	1

	Th	H	T	O
	5	1	3	1
+				

5,131 + 3,051 = ☐

3 Max is working out 3,452 + 42.

a)

	Th	H	T	O
	3	4	5	2
+	4	2		
	7	6	5	2

What mistake has Max made?

_____

_____

b) Work out on the grid the correct answer to Max's question.

	Th	H	T	O
+				

4 What is 2,345 more than 4,153? ⬚

(empty grid)

5 Fill in the missing digits.

a)

	Th	H	T	O
	4	5	1	3
+				
	5	6	5	6

b)

	Th	H	T	O
	3		7	
+		8		6
	7	8	8	7

c)

	Th	H	T	O
	2	1	4	0
+				
	4	8	8	1

d)

	Th	H	T	O
			5	2
+		6		3
	8	9	7	2

6 Complete these calculations. Show which method you used for each.

a) 1,045 + 2,331 = ☐   b) 4,521 + 432 = ☐

7 Find different solutions using only the digits 1 and 8.

CHALLENGE

	Th	H	T	O
+				
	9	9	9	9

	Th	H	T	O
+				
	9	9	9	9

	Th	H	T	O
+				
	9	9	9	9

	Th	H	T	O
+				
	9	9	9	9

Are there more than four solutions?

Reflect

Work out 2,512 + 5,105 using column addition.
Show a partner how you did it.

Date: _____

Add two 4-digit numbers – one exchange

1 **a)** Ebo ran 1,175 m. Lee ran 1,750 m. How far did they run in total?

	Th	H	T	O
		1	1	7	5
+		1	7	5	0

They ran ⬜ m in total.

b) Kate ran 2,400 m and Bella ran 975 m further than Kate. How far did Bella run?

	Th	H	T	O
		2	4	0	0
+			9	7	5

Bella ran ⬜ m.

c) Lexi and Luis both ran 1,245 m. How far did they run altogether?

They ran ⬜ m in total.

	Th	H	T	O
+					

64

2 Solve these additions using the column method.

a) $1,475 + 3,711 =$ ☐

	Th	H	T	O
	1	4	7	5
+	3	7	1	1

c) ☐ $= 1,054 + 5,094$

	Th	H	T	O
+				

b) ☐ $= 3,029 + 2,963$

	Th	H	T	O
+				

d) $179 + 2,608 =$ ☐

	Th	H	T	O
+				

3 Work out

a) $1,575 + 5,520 =$ ☐   b) $1,630 + 3,197 =$ ☐

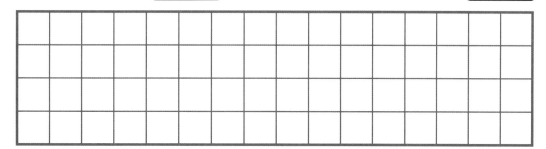

c) Discuss how you can use your answers to work out:

	Th	H	T	O
	4	5	2	0
+	1	5	7	5

	Th	H	T	O
	1	5	6	5
+	5	5	1	0

4) Find the missing digits.

a)

	Th	H	T	O
	1	1	1	1
+				
	2	2	5	0

b)

	Th	H	T	O
+	1	8	2	3
	3	4	5	6

5) Complete the story problem so that it only has an exchange of 10s, and then show the number sentence to solve the problem.

CHALLENGE

There were 1,259 adult tickets sold and ⬚ children's tickets sold.

How many _____?

_____

_____

Reflect

Write three additions that each have one exchange in a different column.

a) 1s

	Th	H	T	O
+				

b) 10s

	Th	H	T	O
+				

c) 100s

	Th	H	T	O
+				

Date: _____   23.2.24

Add with more than one exchange

↓ Textbook 4A p92

1 Complete these additions.

Th	H	T	O
1,000	100 100 100 100 100 100	10 10 10	ı ı ı ı ı
1,000 1,000	100	10 10 10 10 10 / 10 10 10	ı ı ı ı ı / ı

	Th	H	T	O
	1	6	3	5
+	2	1	8	6
	3	8	2	1

Th	H	T	O
1,000 1,000	100 100 100 100	10 10 10 10 10 / 10	ı ı ı ı ı
1,000	100 100 100 100 100 / 100	10 10 10 10 10 / 10	ı ı

	Th	H	T	O
	2	4	6	5
+	1	6	6	2
	4	0	2	7

2 Solve these additions.

a) 1,257 + 189 = ⬚

b) ⬚ = 1,011 + 989

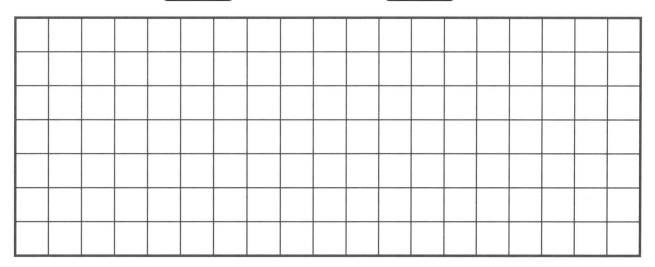

3 Complete these additions. Show your method.

a) 654 + 2,999 = ☐

I can see a mental method.

b) 4,999 + 2,999 = ☐

4 a) Choose pairs of numbers so that each addition has two exchanges. Then solve each of your calculations.

3,405   1,726

1,283   199

	Th	H	T	O
+				

	Th	H	T	O
+				

b) Now think of your own numbers to make up two more additions, each with two exchanges.

	Th	H	T	O
+				

	Th	H	T	O
+				

5 Fill in the missing digits in these calculations.

	Th	H	T	O
	1	2	3	4
+				
	2	0	0	0

	Th	H	T	O
			3	1
+	4		2	
	9	0	0	0

	Th	H	T	O
			0	1
+	1	9		
	9	0	0	0

6 Find the size of each jump below.

CHALLENGE

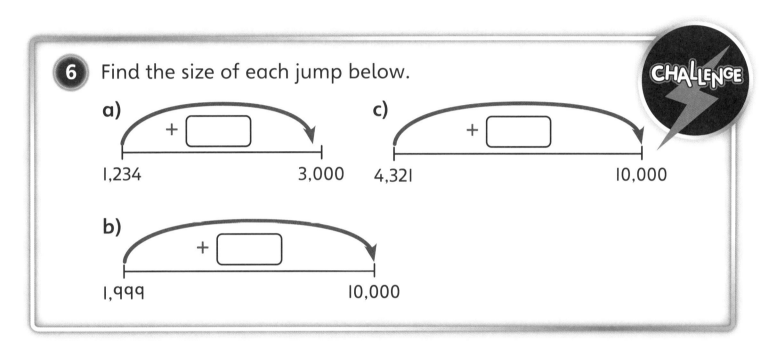

a)

+ ☐

1,234   3,000

c)

+ ☐

4,321   10,000

b)

+ ☐

1,999   10,000

Reflect

Make up an addition that has more than one exchange.

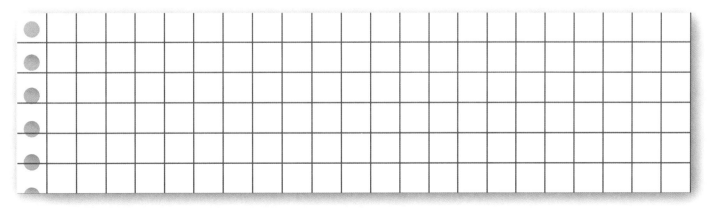

Date: _____

Subtract two 4-digit numbers

1 Work out 4,325 − 2,114.

Th	H	T	O
1,000 1,000 1,000 1,000	100 100 100	10 10	1 1 1 1 1

	Th	H	T	O
	4	3	2	5
⊖	2	1	1	4
	2	2	1	1

2 Solve the subtractions.

a)

	Th	H	T	O
	4	2	5	0
⊖	1	1	4	0
	3	1	1	0

c)

	Th	H	T	O
	4	2	5	2
−	2	0	1	1

b)

	Th	H	T	O
	4	5	2	5
−	2	1	1	4

d)

	Th	H	T	O
	4	5	0	2
−	2	1	0	1

3 Max has £3,568. He spends £2,160 on a sofa.

How much does he have left?

4 Find the missing numbers.

a)

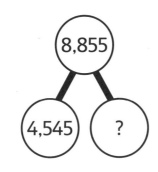

	Th	H	T	O
−				

b)

− 2,550

?   4,999

	Th	H	T	O
−				

c)

9,099

2,066	← ? →

	Th	H	T	O
−				

5 Spot the mistake.

9,732 − 411 = 5,622

Do the correct calculation.

	Th	H	T	O
	9	7	3	2
−		4	1	1
	5	6	2	2

6 Use the digits 5, 5, 6 and 6 to make one odd number and one even number.

Now subtract each of your numbers from 9,999.

9,999 – ⬚ = ⬚   9,999 – ⬚ = ⬚

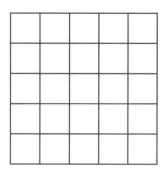   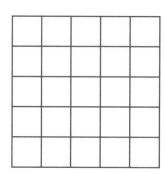

What do you notice about whether the answers are odd or even?

I noticed that _____

_____

_____

_____

Reflect

Write and solve a story problem for 5,455 – 2,123.

- _____
- _____
- _____
- _____

Subtract two 4-digit numbers – one exchange

1 Complete the subtractions.

a) 4,362 − 247 = ☐

Th	H	T	O
1,000 1,000 1,000 1,000	100 100 100	10 10 10 10 10 / 10	/ /

	Th	H	T	O
	4	3	⁵6̶ ⁵2	
⊖		2	4	7
	4	1	1	5

b) 1,454 − 1,270 = ☐

Th	H	T	O
1,000	100 100 100 100	10 10 10 10 10	/ / / /

	Th	H	T	O
	1	¹4̶	⁵5	4
⊖	1	2	7	0
	0	1	8	4

c) 2,350 − 1,530 = ☐

Th	H	T	O
1,000 1,000	100 100 100	10 10 10 10 10	

	Th	H	T	O
	¹2̶	¹3	5	0
⊖	1	5	3	0
	0	8	2	0

2 Kate lives 349 metres away from work.

Bella lives 1,356 metres away from work.

How much further from work does Bella live than Kate?

Bella lives ☐1,007 metres further away.

	Th	H	T	O
	1	3	⁴5̶	¹6
⊖		3	4	9
	1	0	0	7

3 Complete these subtractions.

a) 9,375 − 8,293 = ☐

	Th	H	T	O
−				

c) 9,375 − 8,239 = ☐

	Th	H	T	O
−				

b) ☐ = 8,375 − 8,293

	Th	H	T	O
−				

d) 7,375 − 239 = ☐

	Th	H	T	O
−				

4 Find the missing numbers.

a)

Th	H	T	O
1,000 1,000 1,000 1,000	100 100	10 10 10 10 10	1 1

	Th	H	T	O
	4	2	5	2
−				
	2	1	1	3

b)

Th	H	T	O
1,000 1,000	100 100 100 100 100	10 10 10	1

	Th	H	T	O
	2	5	3	1
−				
		9	1	1

5 Calculate the missing digits.

CHALLENGE

a)

	Th	H	T	O
	1	8	7	2
−	1		4	
			7	8

b)

	Th	H	T	O
	2	8	9	1
−				
		9	5	0

c)

	Th	H	T	O
	3			6
−		2	6	2
	2	4	5	

d)

	Th	H	T	O
−	3	6	6	1
	4	1	2	8

Reflect

Write and solve a subtraction that needs an exchange of 1 hundred for 10 tens.

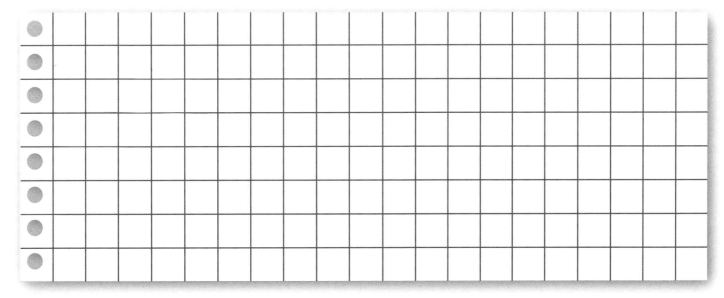

Date: __2·2·24__

Subtract two 4-digit numbers – more than one exchange

1 Max scored 2,335 points in a game. Isla scored 418 fewer points. How many points did Isla score?

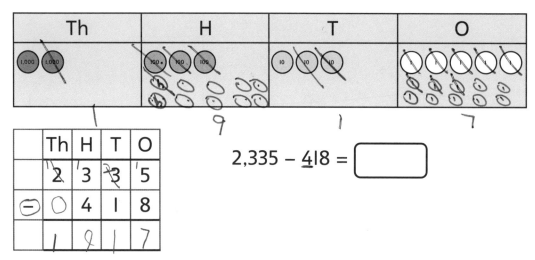

	Th	H	T	O
	²2	3	²3	⁵5
⊖	0	4	1	8
		1	9	1	7

2,335 – 4̲18 = [   ]

Isla scored [   ] points.

2 Complete these subtractions.

a) 2,292 – 1,199 = [   ]

	Th	H	T	O
	2	¹2	⁸9	¹2
⊖	1	1	9	9
		1	0	9	3

b) [   ] = 3,150 – 1,160

	Th	H	T	O
	²3	⁰0̸	¹5	0
⊖	1	1	6	0
		1	7	9	0

c) 1,251 – 182 = [   ]

	Th	H	T	O
		1	2	5	1
–			1	8	2

d) 3,150 – 225 = [   ]

	Th	H	T	O
		3	1	5	0
–			2	2	5

3 Explain the mistake and show the correct calculation.

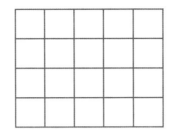

	Th	H	T	O
	3	4	1	2
−	1	6	5	1
	2	2	4	1

The mistake is that _____

_____

4 Work out these calculations.

a) 1,258 litres − 163 litres

	Th	H	T	O
−				

c) £3,215 − £329

	Th	H	T	O
−				

b) 5,392 kg − 1,628 kg

	Th	H	T	O
−				

d) 6,500 km − 2,970 km

	Th	H	T	O
−				

5 1,☐58 − 28☐ has two exchanges.

What could the missing digits be?

	Th	H	T	O
−				

6 Richard thinks that the rabbit's mass is closer to the cat's mass than it is to the guinea pig's mass.

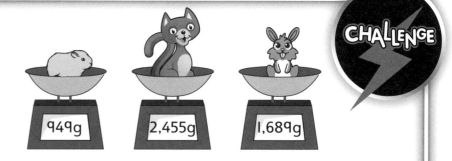

Do you agree with Richard? Explain your answer.

Reflect

Write down a calculation you think has two exchanges.

Ask a partner to check.

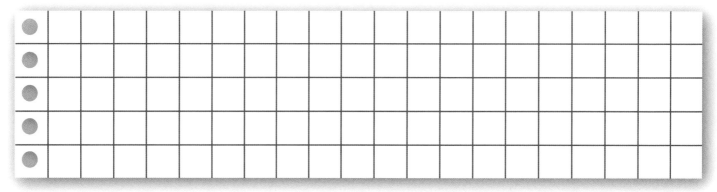

Date: _____

Exchange across two columns

1 Solve each of the subtractions.

a) 2,502 – 1,359 = ☐

	Th	H	T	O
–				

c) 3,026 – 573 = ☐

	Th	H	T	O
–				

b) 4,506 – 1,482 = ☐

	Th	H	T	O
–				

d) 8,017 – 1,928 = ☐

	Th	H	T	O
–				

2 Olivia is reading a story that is 1,401 words long.

She has read 225 words so far.

How many words does she have left to read?

	Th	H	T	O
–				

☐ words

3 David has £5,048. He spends £2,362 on a family holiday.

How much money does he have left?

	Th	H	T	O
–				

£ ☐

79

4 Max has completed some subtractions.

Correct any mistakes he has made.

	Th	H	T	O
	3	5	¹0	¹7
−		4	1	9
	3	1	9	8

	Th	H	T	O
	²3̶	⁹¹0̶	⁹¹0̶	¹8
−	1	4	1	9
	1	5	9	9

	Th	H	T	O
	¹2̶	¹0	¹2̶	¹3
−		4	1	9
	1	6	0	4

5 Solve each subtraction.

a) 7,002 − 1,359 = ☐

c) 5,011 − 827 = ☐

b) 3,006 − 2,478 = ☐

d) 9,023 − 3,624 = ☐

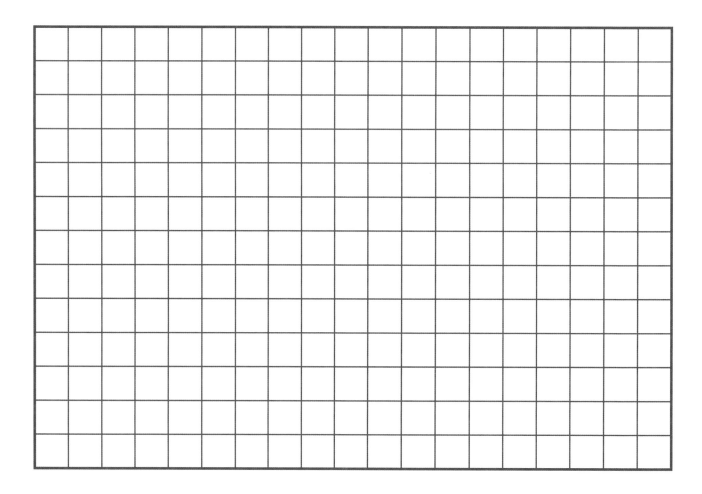

6 Calculate the missing parts.

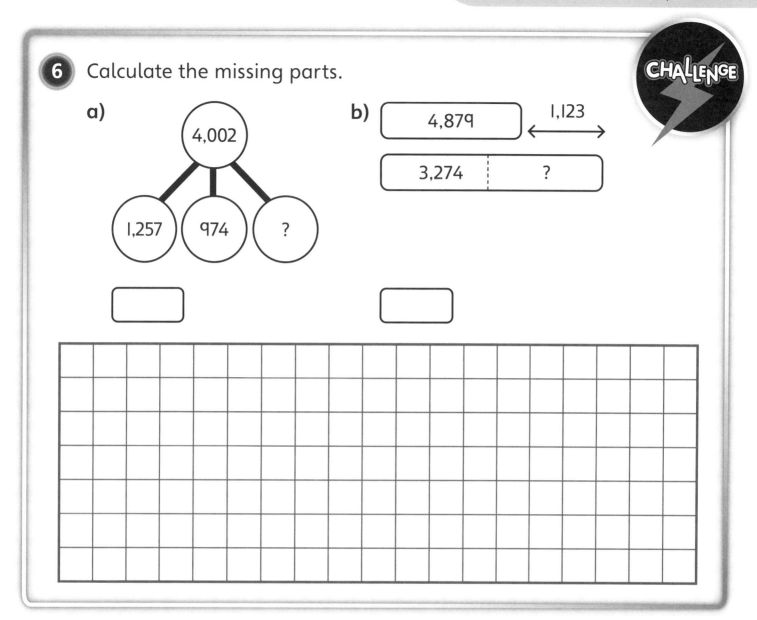

a)

4,002

1,257   974   ?

b)

4,879   1,123 ⟷

3,274   ?

CHALLENGE

Reflect

Explain how to make an exchange for 10 ones when there is zero in the tens column.

Date: _____

Efficient methods

1 Solve each calculation.

a) $1{,}957 + 1{,}000 =$ ⬚

   $1{,}957 + 999 \;=$ ⬚

b) $3{,}175 + 1{,}000 =$ ⬚

   $3{,}175 + 999 \;=$ ⬚

c) $1{,}957 - 1{,}000 =$ ⬚

   $1{,}957 - 999 \;=$ ⬚

d) $3{,}175 - 1{,}000 =$ ⬚

   $3{,}175 - 999 \;=$ ⬚

e) $2{,}048 + 1{,}000 =$ ⬚

   $2{,}048 + 999 \;=$ ⬚

f) $8{,}858 + 1{,}000 =$ ⬚

   $8{,}858 + 999 \;=$ ⬚

g) $2{,}048 - 1{,}000 =$ ⬚

   $2{,}048 - 999 \;=$ ⬚

h) $8{,}858 - 1{,}000 =$ ⬚

   $8{,}858 - 999 \;=$ ⬚

2 Solve each calculation.

a) $1{,}582 + 1{,}999 \;=$ ⬚

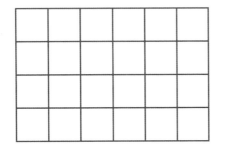

b) $3{,}999 + 1{,}672 =$ ⬚

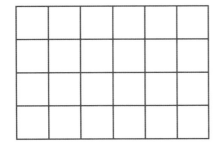

c) $4{,}316 - 2{,}999 =$ ⬚

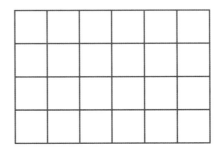

d) $7{,}072 - 5{,}999 \;=$ ⬚

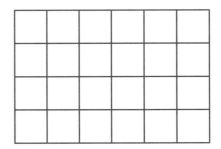

3 Solve each calculation.

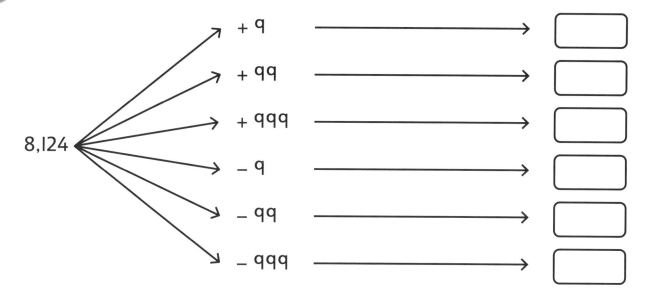

8,124
+ 9
+ 99
+ 999
– 9
– 99
– 999

4 Show the mental method you would use for each of these calculations.

a) $3,251 - 6 =$ ▢

c) $3,251 - 3,246 =$ ▢

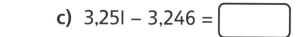

3,251   3,251

b) $5,051 -$ ▢ $= 4$

d) $4,982 = 4,982 -$ ▢

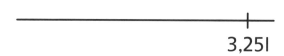

5 Choose a suitable method and solve each calculation.

a) 9,706 − 998 = ⬚

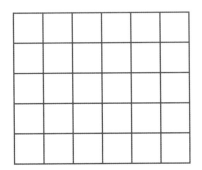

c) 5,002 − 4,894 = ⬚

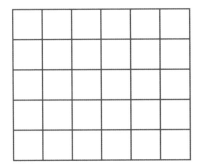

b) 1,200 − 3 = ⬚

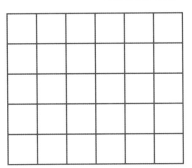

d) 4,836 − 2,754 = ⬚

Reflect

a) Write a calculation you would solve using a written method.

b) Write a calculation you would solve using a mental method.

Equivalent difference

1 Write a subtraction to go with each model.

Complete all the subtractions. What do you notice?

→ Textbook 4A p116

a)
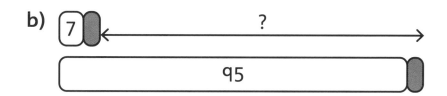

	H	T	O
−			

b)
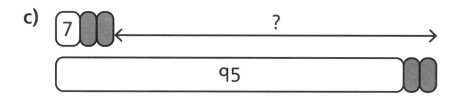

	H	T	O
−			

c)
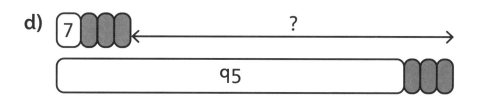

	H	T	O
−			

d)

	H	T	O
−			

e) What did you notice about your answers?

Which calculation was easiest? Discuss.

2 Use the bar model to work out 298 − 139 = [ ].

Write the subtraction you used.

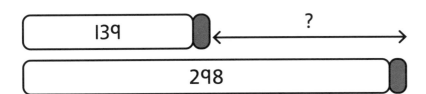

	H	T	O
−			

3 Jan's tower is 235 cm tall.

Anne's is 98 cm tall.

Write subtractions to find the difference between the height of the towers.

Tick the one you choose to complete first.

	H	T	O
	2	3	5
−		9	8

	H	T	O
	2	3	6
−			

	H	T	O
−			

	H	T	O
−			

	H	T	O
−			

[ ]'s tower is [ ] cm taller.

4 Ebo solved 2,001 − 567 = [ ] with the calculation.

1,999 − 565 = [ ].

Complete his calculation to find the answer.

	Th	H	T	O
	1	9	9	9
−		5	6	5

86

5 Choose a suitable method and solve each of these subtractions. Think about which method is the most efficient each time.

a) 2,950 − 850 = ⬚

d) 8,001 − 4,567 = ⬚

b) 2,875 − 1,989 = ⬚

e) 6,626 − 6,618 = ⬚

c) 3,011 − 2,997 = ⬚

f) 9,009 − 10 = ⬚

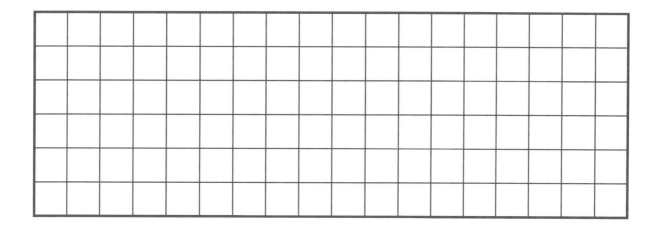

Reflect

Think of another method to solve 1,000 − 955.

Discuss with a partner which you think is most efficient.

	Th	H	T	O
	1	0	0	0
−		9	5	5

I think the best method is to _____

_____

because _____

_____

Date: _____

Estimate answers

1 Estimate the answers by rounding to the nearest 1,000.

a) Max scores 3,987 points in a game. Lexi scores 5,123 points more than Max. Estimate Lexi's score.

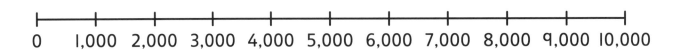

0   1,000   2,000   3,000   4,000   5,000   6,000   7,000   8,000   9,000   10,000

3,987 rounds to ☐,000   5,123 rounds to ☐,000

Estimate: ☐ + ☐ = ☐

Lexi's score is roughly ☐,000 points.

b) Max loses 3,104 points. Estimate how many points he has now.

Estimate: ☐ − ☐ = ☐

Max has roughly ☐ points now.

c) Now work out the exact scores and compare them with your estimates.

Lexi's exact score

Th	H	T	O

Max's exact score

Th	H	T	O

How close are your estimates to the exact answers?

2 Join each calculation to the estimate that best matches it.

Calculations

| 2,101 – 998 |

| 1,975 + 2,010 |

| 1,998 + 3,101 |

| 2,925 – 975 |

| 2,998 – 1,998 |

Estimates

| 2,000 + 2,000 |

| 3,000 – 2,000 |

| 2,100 – 1,000 |

| 3,000 – 1,000 |

| 2,000 + 3,000 |

3 **a)** Complete each calculation. Then write an estimate to check.

6,152 + 3,025 = [ ]

6,452 – 2,005 = [ ]

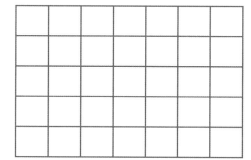

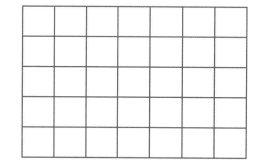

Estimate:

[ ] + [ ] = [ ]

Estimate:

[ ] – [ ] = [ ]

b) Explain why you chose each of your estimation methods.

_____

_____

_____

4 6,491 − 2,725 = [   ]

CHALLENGE

Estimate the answer by rounding to the nearest 1,000.
Then estimate by rounding to the nearest 100.
Then estimate by rounding to the nearest 10.

Nearest 1,000	Nearest 100	Nearest 10
Estimate: [ ]	Estimate: [ ]	Estimate: [ ]

Find the exact answers and compare them to your estimates.

What do you notice?

Th	H	T	O

_____

_____

_____

Reflect

Explain how you would estimate 1,915 − 1,019.

- _____
- _____
- _____
- _____

Check strategies

↓ Textbook 4A p124

1 Check Emma's subtractions using the inverse operation.

Complete the part-whole models to help you.

a) Emma has got this answer

$3{,}412 - 1{,}151 = 2{,}341$

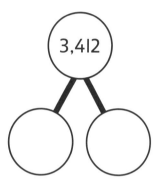

	Th	H	T	O
		2	3	4	1
+				

b) Emma has got this answer

$1{,}001 - 550 = 451$

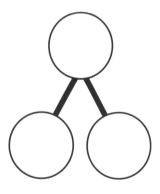

	Th	H	T	O

c) Emma has got this answer

$9{,}876 - 6{,}789 = 2{,}189$

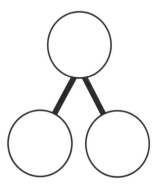

	Th	H	T	O

2 Holly bought a car for £1,899.

She also paid £995 to get it repaired.

Holly has calculated that she spent £2,894 in total.

Show that Holly is correct. Check your answer using a subtraction.

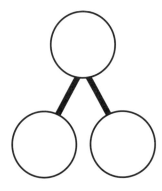

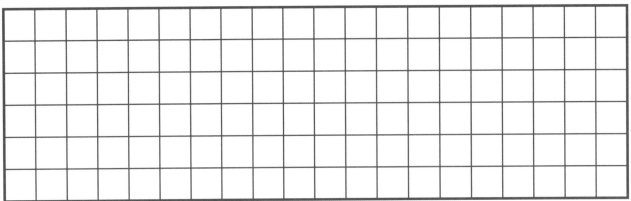

3 Calculate the missing numbers.

a) [　　] + 995 = 5,555

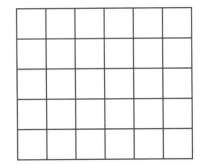

c) 5,555 − [　　] = 995

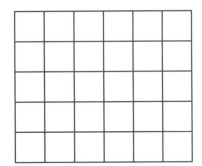

b) [　　] − 5,555 = 995

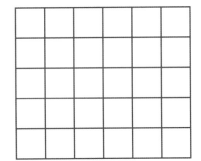

d) [　　] − 995 = [　　]

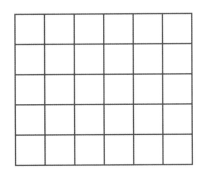

4 $4,499 + 3,499 = 7,998$

Do you agree with Dexter that his estimate is not right?

Explain how you would check this calculation.

CHALLENGE

> I rounded to estimate $4,000 + 3,000 = 7,000$, but the answer rounds to $8,000$ so I do not think my estimate is right.

_____

_____

_____

_____

Reflect

Show how to check $599 + 1,599 = 2,098$.

Date: _____

Problem solving – one step

1 Ambika poured 2,500 ml of water onto a flower bed.

Aki poured 3,100 ml of water.

a) How much water did they pour altogether?

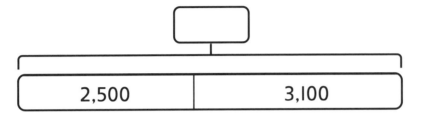

	Th	H	T	O
+				

b) Ambika started with 5,000 ml in her watering can.

How much water does she have left now?

	Th	H	T	O
+				

2 **a)** Mrs Dean lives 5,000 m from her school. She has cycled 3,900 m so far. How far does she have left to cycle?

Use the bar model to show the problem and then answer it.

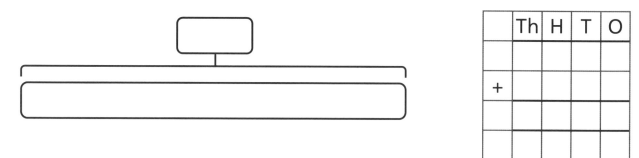

	Th	H	T	O
+				

b) Mr Jones walks 1,250 m to the bus stop, then travels 2,900 m on the bus. How far does he travel altogether?

Draw a bar model to show the problem and then answer it.

3 Draw bar models and find the missing numbers.

a) $\boxed{} - 3{,}750 = 4{,}000$

b) $4{,}000 - \boxed{} = 3{,}750$

95

4 Crack the code.

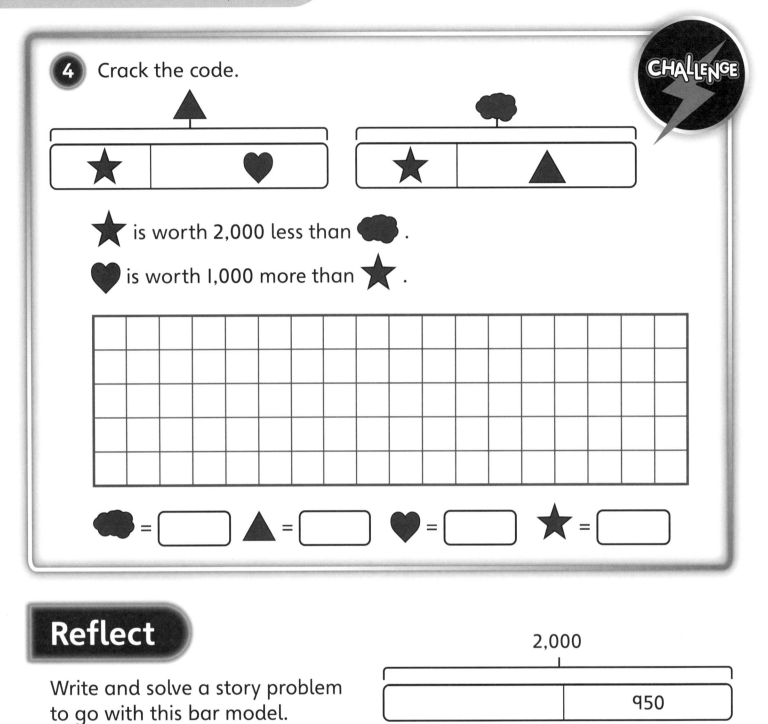

★ is worth 2,000 less than ☁.

♥ is worth 1,000 more than ★.

☁ = ☐   ▲ = ☐   ♥ = ☐   ★ = ☐

Reflect

Write and solve a story problem
to go with this bar model.

2,000

	950

Problem solving – comparison

1 **a)** Ebo has 1,020 football stickers. Richard has 820 football stickers.

How many more stickers does Ebo have than Richard?

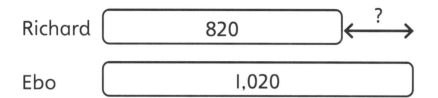

Richard | 820 | ? |

Ebo | 1,020 |

	Th	H	T	O
	⁰/	¹0	2	0
−		8	2	0
		2	0	0

Ebo has [200] more stickers than Richard.

b) Reena has 1,500 stickers. How many fewer stickers does Ebo have than Reena?

Reena | 1,500 |

Ebo

	Th	H	T	O
+				

Ebo has [ ] fewer stickers than Reena.

c) Luis has 250 more stickers than Reena. Show this on a bar model and work out how many stickers Luis has in total.

Luis

Reena

Luis has [ ] stickers in total.

97

2 Mo collects 425 shells and Lee collects 576 shells.

How many more shells does Lee collect than Mo?

Explain which bar model suits this problem.

A

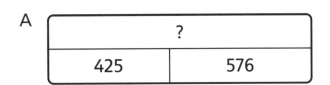

B

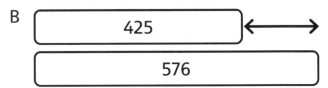

I think [A] / [B] suits this problem better because _____

_____

_____

_____

3 Draw a bar model and solve this problem.

Max has 1,500 ml of paint. Isla has 750 ml more paint than Max.

Max uses 500 ml of paint. Isla also uses some paint and now they have the same amount of paint left as each other.

How much paint did Isla use?

4 Solve this story problem by drawing bar models.

CHALLENGE

Bella, Aki and Andy each think of a number.

Bella's number is 875 more than Aki's number.

Aki subtracts 499 from his number.

Now Aki's number is 245 less than Andy's number.

What is the difference between Bella's number and Andy's number?

The difference between Bella's number and Andy's number

is [   ] .

Reflect

I would draw a comparison bar model when _____

_____

I would draw a single bar model when _____

_____

Date: __3·4·24__

Problem solving – two steps

1 **a)** Sofia entered a <u>triathlon</u>. She swam 500 m, cycled 2,250 m and ran 1,250 m to the finish.

What was the total distance?

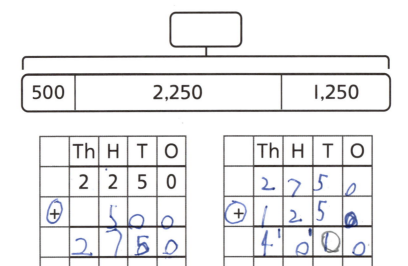

| | 500 | 2,250 | 1,250 |

Th	H	T	O
	2	2	5	0
+		5	0	0
	2	7	5	0

Th	H	T	O
	2	7	5	0
+	1	2	5	0
	4	0	0	0

b) Mrs Dean entered an 8,000 m triathlon. She ran 2,500 m and cycled <u>4,750 m</u>.

How far did she swim?

8,000

| 2500 | 4750 | 7550 ? 1000 |

7000

①	4	7	5	0			
+	2	5	0	0			
	7	2	5	0	+		

= 8 0 0 0

② 7 2 5 0

0 7 5 0

2 What is the height of the middle section of the tower?

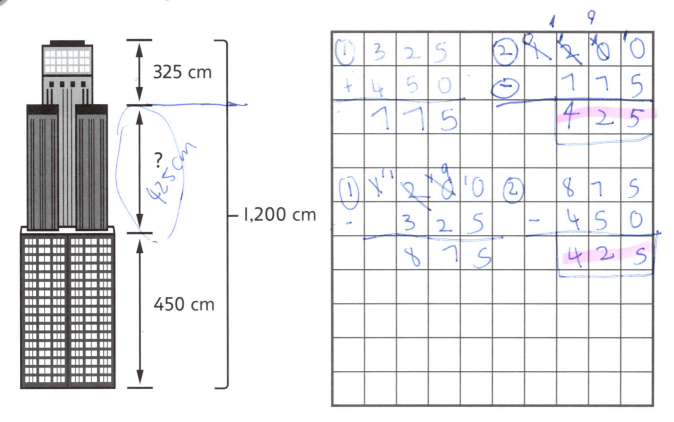

325 cm

? cm
425 cm

1,200 cm

450 cm

① 3 2 5
+ 4 5 0
7 7 5

② 1,200
    - 7 7 5
      4 2 5

① 1,200
  - 3 2 5
    8 7 5

② 8 7 5
  - 4 5 0
    4 2 5

3 Draw a bar model and solve this story problem.

There are 650 children in a primary school.

There are 1,100 more children in the secondary school. than in the PS.

How many children are there in total? ☐

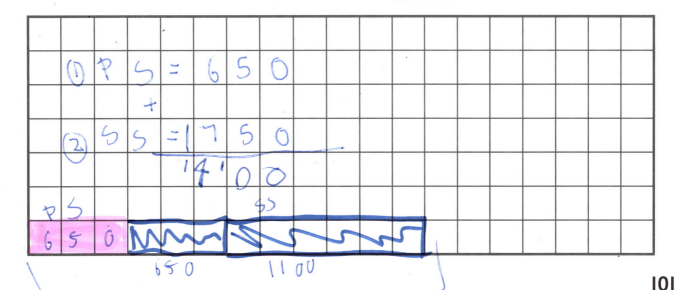

① P S = 6 5 0
      +
② S S = 1 7 5 0
      1 4 0 0   SS

P S
6 5 0

650   1100

4 **a)** Amy has £1,275 less than her brother Ben.
Then Ben spends £550 and Amy gets £750.
Who has more money now? What is the difference
between the amounts that Amy and Ben now have?

CHALLENGE

_____ has more money now.

The difference is £ ⬚ .

b) Evelyn has £800 more than Noah. Together they have £2,800.
How much do they each have?

Evelyn has £ ⬚ and Noah has £ ⬚ .

Reflect

Draw a bar model with three parts that total 2,050.

Problem solving – multi-step problems

1 Mr Jones's school collected 5,000 bottles for a recycling competition.

- Class 1 collected 1,228 bottles.
- Class 3 collected 1,517 bottles.
- Class 4 collected 483 bottles.
- Class 2 think they collected the most bottles.

a) Complete both diagrams to show this problem.

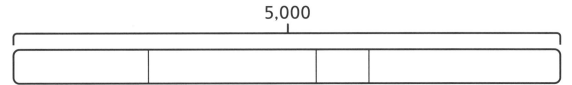

5,000

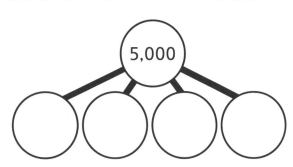

5,000

b) Calculate how many bottles Class 2 collected.

Which class collected the most bottles?

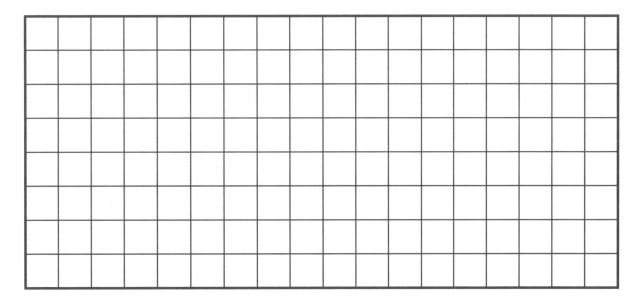

103

2 There are 3,985 United fans at a football match and 1,700 fewer Rovers fans.

How many fans are there in total?

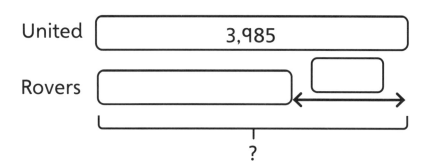

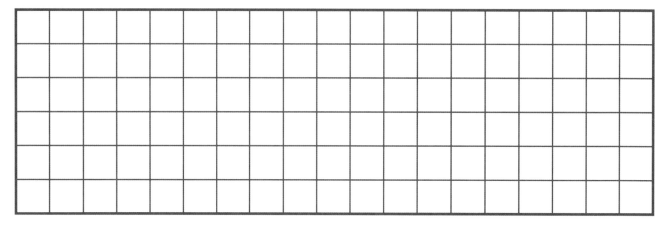

3 The mass of a rabbit is 1,502 g.

The mass of a hamster is 4,586 g less than the mass of a small dog.

The mass of a small dog is 3,116 g more than the mass of rabbit.

What is the mass of the hamster?

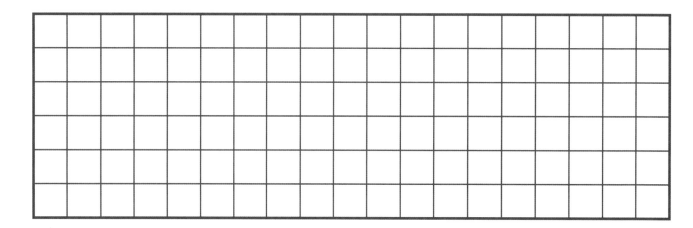

4 Write a story problem to match the diagram.

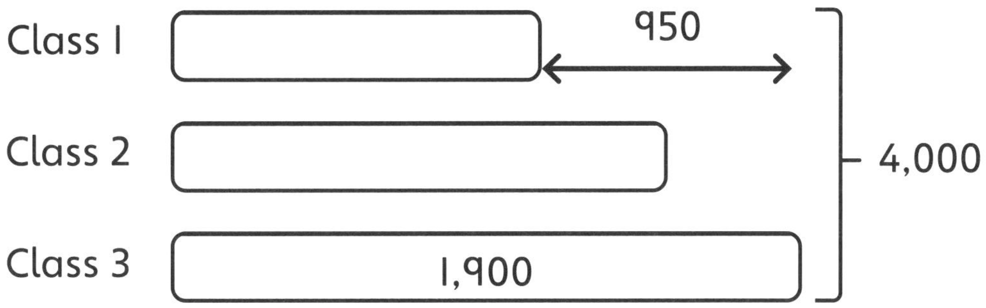

CHALLENGE

Class 1 | [ ] ←— 950 —→ ⎤
Class 2 | [ ]   ⎟— 4,000
Class 3 | [1,900] ⎦

_____

_____

_____

_____

_____

_____

_____

Reflect

When I draw a bar model to help me solve a problem, I decide

how many bars I need to draw by _____

_____

_____

Date: _____

End of unit check

My journal

↑ Textbook 4A p144

1    $1,849 + \boxed{} = 8,634$ $2,026 = 9,000 - \boxed{}$

Isla knows that one of these calculations has a missing number greater than **6,800**, but she cannot remember which one it is.

Make a prediction and explain how you chose it.

Then show how to complete each calculation accurately.

_____

_____

_____

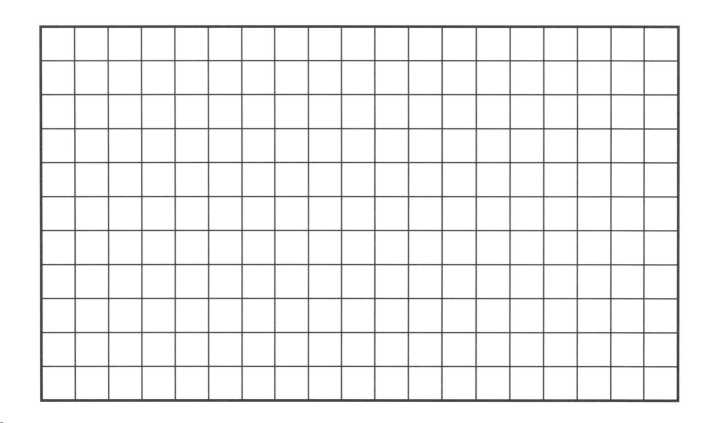

2 Aki, Jamilla and Lee are playing a game.

Aki scores 4,875 points.

Lee scores 8,699 points.

Jamilla scores 3,823 less than Aki.

Aki thinks his score is closer to Lee's score than it is to Jamilla's score.

Explain whether or not Aki is correct. You may use diagrams to explain.

_____

_____

_____

Power check

How do you feel about your work in this unit?

Power puzzle

What is the value of each shape?

Puzzle A

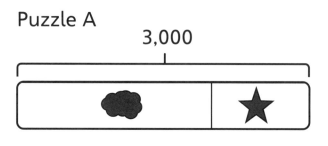

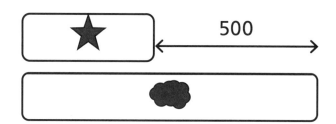

Puzzle B

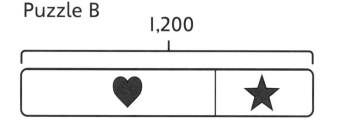

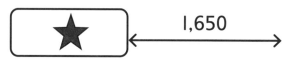

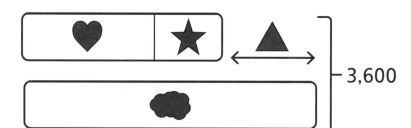

Create your own puzzle like this for a partner to solve. Choose two numbers and draw the bar model. Show your partner the total and the difference but hide the numbers from them.

What is area?

1 Use counters to estimate the area of the square.

The area of the square is

about ⬜ counters.

2 The area of these shapes has been measured in different ways.

Complete the measurements for each shape.

a) The area of this quadrilateral

is about ⬜ dominoes.

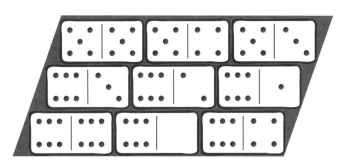

b) The area of this triangle

is about ⬜ buttons.

↓ Textbook 4A p148

109

3 Explain what area is in your own words.

_____

_____

4 Use counters to estimate the area of each shape.

a)

counters

b)

counters

c)

counters

5 Tick all of the examples that could be used to show area.

The number of children that can sit on a mat.

The number of potato prints that cover a piece of paper.

The number of steps it takes to walk around the outside of a field.

The number of bathroom tiles that cover a wall.

6 Mo has estimated the area of a rectangle using sticky notes.

CHALLENGE

a) Mo says, 'The area of the rectangle is about 24 sticky notes.'

Explain the mistake Mo has made.

_____

_____

b) Estimate the area of the rectangle.

There are ☐ sticky notes.

Reflect

Use objects to estimate the area of the front of your Power Maths textbook. Did you use the same objects as a partner? Did you get the same area?

I estimate the area to be ☐.

What objects did you use?

Date: _____

Measure area using squares

1 Count the squares to find the area of each shape.

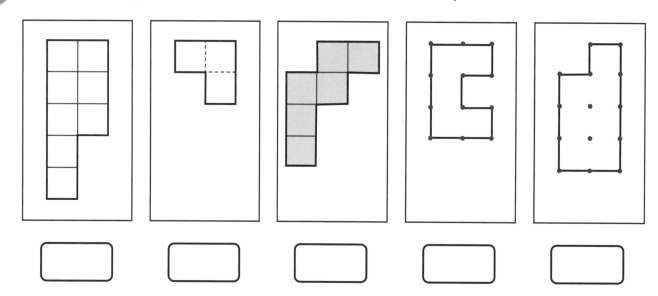

2 a) Complete the table below to show the areas.

Shape	A	B	C	D	E
Area (squares)					

b) Shapes ⬚ and ⬚ have the same area.

3 Georgia is measuring the area of a piece of paper. She fits exactly 2 rows of 4 squares inside the shape.

What is the area of the piece of paper?

The area of the piece of paper is ☐ squares.

4 Ebo has filled this rectangle in with squares. He says this shows it has an area of 7 squares.

Discuss with a partner the mistake Ebo has made.

5 Crack the code to spell the name of an object. Count the squares in the shapes below to find the letters. Then measure the area of the object.

KEY: I square = A   2 squares = B   3 squares = E   4 squares = F
5 squares = L   6 squares = O   7 squares = P   8 squares = T

6 Here is a sequence of squares.

CHALLENGE

a) Write the area underneath each shape.

b) What will be the areas of the next three shapes in the sequence?

_____

_____

_____

c) Discuss with a partner how you can find the answers without drawing the shapes.

Reflect

Why would you use squares to measure area?

_____

_____

_____

Count squares

1 Here is a plan of a child's bedroom.

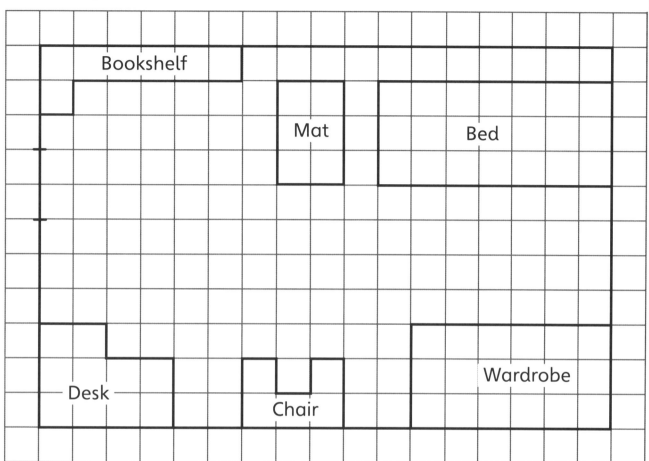

a) Complete the table to show the area of each object on the plan.

b) Draw your own object on the plan and in the last line of the table write down its area.

Object	Area (squares)
Desk	
Chair	
Wardrobe	
Mat	
Bookshelf	
Bed	
_____	

115

2 Look at the shapes and complete the statements.

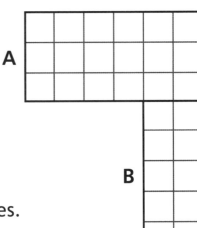

Rectangle A has an area of ⬚ squares.

Rectangle B has an area of ⬚ squares.

Area of A + B = ⬚ squares + ⬚ squares = ⬚ squares

The whole shape has an area of ⬚ squares.

3 A shape is made up of two rectangles joined together.

Draw your shape then work out its area.

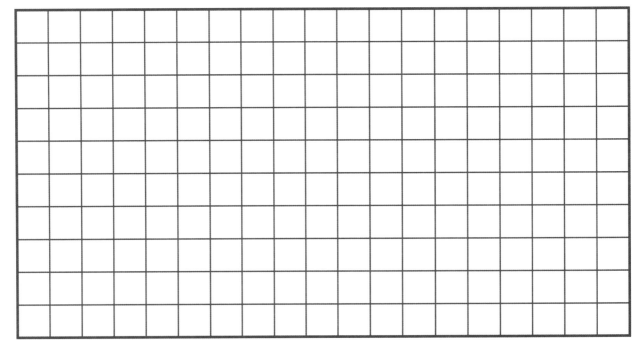

Total area = ⬚ squares + ⬚ squares = ⬚ squares

4 Some ink has been spilled on a rectangle.

What is the area of the rectangle?

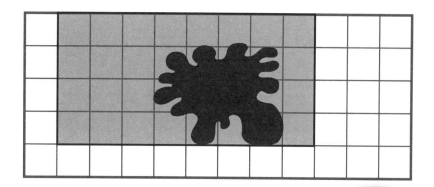

[ ] squares

5 A farmer wants to split his land into 5 fields, all the same area.

On the map, the shaded square shows the farmhouse and the rest of the squares show the area of the land around it.

Draw lines on the map to show how he can split up his land.

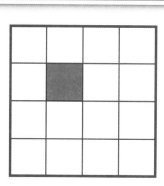

Map of Oak Farm

CHALLENGE

I have found a way to do this where the fields are all the same shape, too!

Reflect

Discuss with a partner how to find the area of this rectangle. Discuss two different ways.

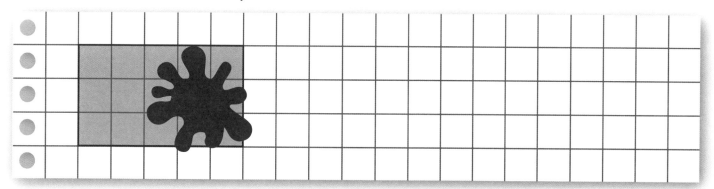

Date: _____

Make shapes

1 Draw four different shapes with an area of 6 squares.

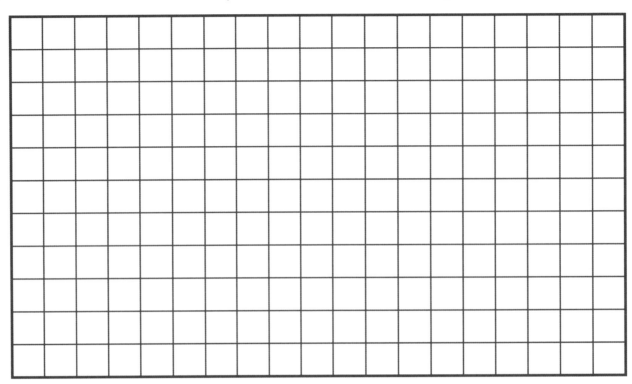

2 Draw two different rectilinear shapes, each with an area of 20 squares.

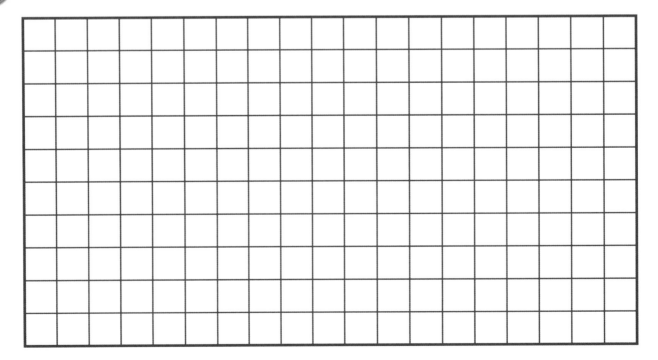

118

3 Count the squares to find the area of each shape.

a)

b)

c)

d)

☐ squares   ☐ squares   ☐ squares   ☐ squares

4 Create two of your initials with squares then answer the questions.

a) Write down the area of each letter underneath it.

b) Which letter has the largest area? _____

c) What is the total area of your initials? ☐ squares

_____

_____

_____

_____

CHALLENGE

5 Shade in squares to make your own design.

What is the area of your design?

[   ] squares

I will design a spaceship.

Reflect

Kyle is learning how to make different rectilinear shapes out of the same number of squares.

Write three rules to help him to know what to do.

1. _____

2. _____

3. _____

Date: _____

Compare area

1 Abdul, Bryony and Chloe have finished playing a game.

The winner is the person who has made the shape with the largest area.

a) Without counting, who do you think has won the game?

_____

b) Now count the squares to complete the table.

Player	Area of shape
Abdul	⬚
Bryony	⬚
Chloe	⬚

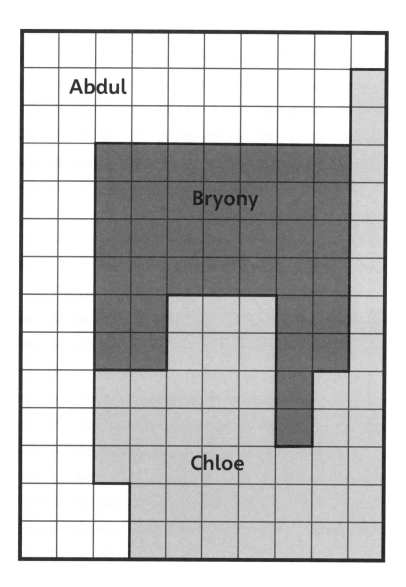

c) Who has won the game? Explain how you know.

_____

_____

121

↓ Textbook 4A p164

2 Look carefully at the shapes on this board.

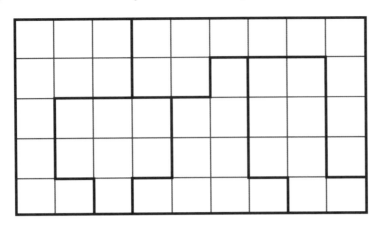

a) Label the shape with the smallest area A.

b) Label the shape with the greatest area B.

c) The area of the whole board is ⬜ squares.

3 Write the area of each shape in the box underneath, then shade in the shape with the larger area in each pair.

a)

⬜ squares   ⬜ squares

c)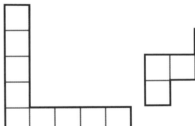

⬜ squares   ⬜ squares

b)

⬜ squares   ⬜ square

d)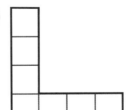

⬜ squares   ⬜ squares

4 Draw a rectangle that has an area double the area of this shape.

CHALLENGE

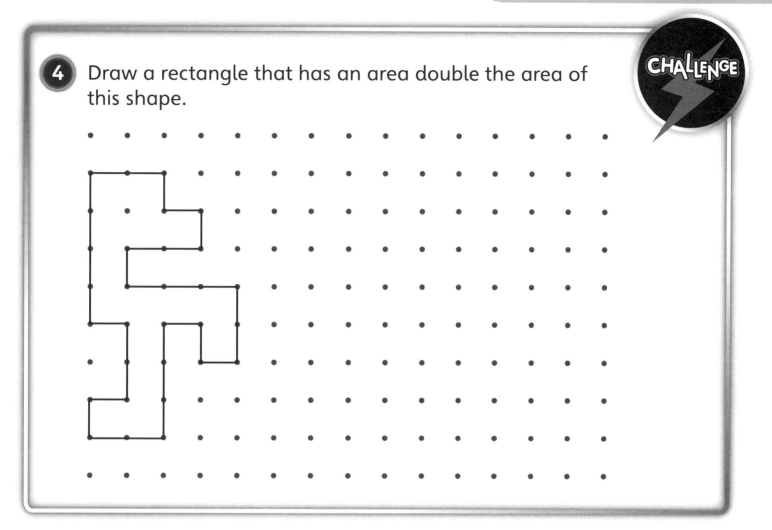

Reflect

'Rectangles have a larger area than squares.'

Is this statement always true, sometimes true or never true?

Explain your reasoning.

End of unit check

My journal

↑ Textbook 4A p168

1 Draw three different shapes, each with an area of 12 squares.

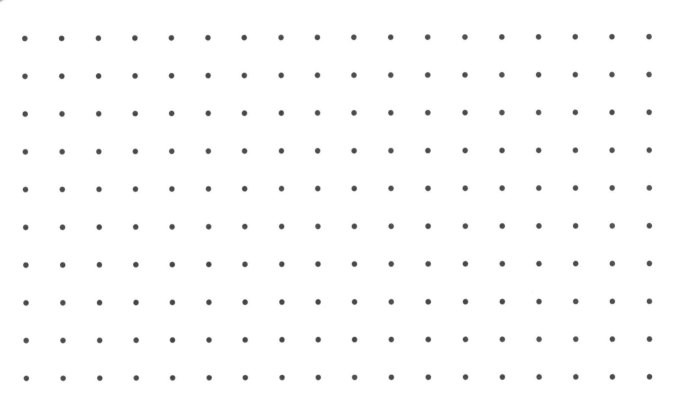

2 Explain how you decided the measurements for your shapes.

_____

_____

Power check

How do you feel about your work in this unit?

Power play

Aaron has dropped 2 chocolate bars on the floor.

They have broken into 8 pieces.

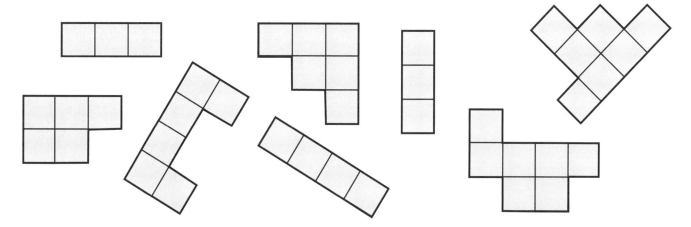

Use square dotted paper to copy and cut out each of these 8 shapes.

a) The two chocolate bars were both squares, but they had different areas. Move your shapes around to make two rectangles.

b) The areas of the chocolate bars are ⬚ squares and ⬚ squares.

c) Which bar would you choose and why? Use the word 'area' in your answer.

_____

_____

_____

Make your own puzzle by cutting up two rectangles. Give a partner a clue about the rectangles. Can they find the areas?

Date: _____

Multiples of 3

1 **a)** Draw 3 groups of 5.

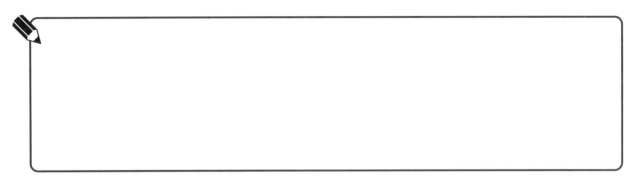

b) Draw 5 groups of 3.

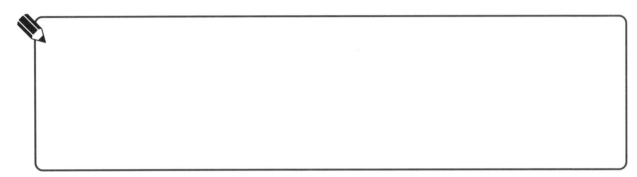

c) Complete each calculation.

$3 \times 5 = \boxed{}$ $\boxed{} \div 3 = 5$

$5 \times 3 = \boxed{}$ $\boxed{} \div 5 = 3$

2 Write two multiplications and two divisions for each array.

$\boxed{} \times \boxed{} = \boxed{}$ $\boxed{} \div \boxed{} = \boxed{}$

$\boxed{} \times \boxed{} = \boxed{}$ $\boxed{} \div \boxed{} = \boxed{}$

$\boxed{} \times \boxed{} = \boxed{}$ $\boxed{} \div \boxed{} = \boxed{}$

$\boxed{} \times \boxed{} = \boxed{}$ $\boxed{} \div \boxed{} = \boxed{}$

3 Complete the triangle and write four facts.

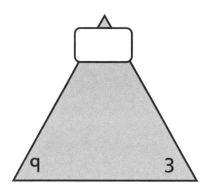

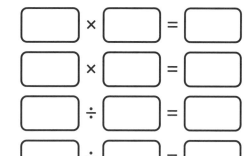

4 Solve each calculation.

Use the space to draw or make anything that helps.

a) $9 \div 3 = \boxed{}$

b) $24 \div 3 = \boxed{}$

5 Complete the multiples of 3.

0   3   6   [ ] [ ] [ ] [ ] [ ] [ ] [ ]   30

6 Colour all the squares holding multiples of 3.

CHALLENGE

1	2	3	4	5	6	7	8	9	10
11	12	13	14	15	16	17	18	19	20
21	22	23	24	25	26	27	28	29	30
31	32	33	34	35	36	37	38	39	40
41	42	43	44	45	46	47	48	49	50
51	52	53	54	55	56	57	58	59	60
61	62	63	64	65	66	67	68	69	70
71	72	73	74	75	76	77	78	79	80
81	82	83	84	85	86	87	88	89	90
91	92	93	94	95	96	97	98	99	100

What do you notice?

_____

_____

_____

_____

_____

_____

Reflect

Which number is a multiple of 3: [23] [13] [27] ? How do you know?

_____

_____

_____

_____

Multiply and divide by 6

→ Textbook 4A p176

 a) $3 \times 6 = \boxed{}$

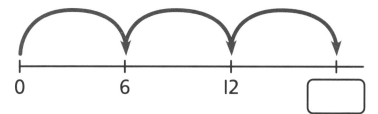

0   6   12 $\boxed{}$

b) $5 \times 6 = \boxed{}$

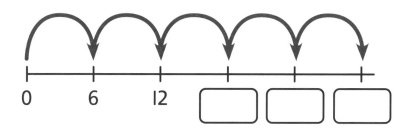

0   6   12 $\boxed{}$ $\boxed{}$ $\boxed{}$

c) $10 \times 6 = \boxed{}$

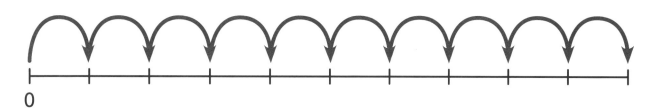

0

2 $24 \div 6 = \boxed{}$

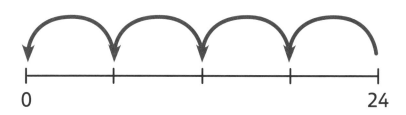

0   24

3 **a)** How many pears are there in total?

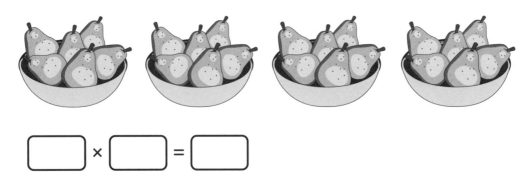

$\boxed{} \times \boxed{} = \boxed{}$

b) How many flowers are there in total?

$\boxed{} \times \boxed{} = \boxed{}$

4 Alex has 48 triangles.

6 triangles are put together to make a hexagon.

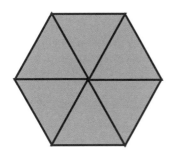

How many hexagons can Alex make in total?

$\boxed{} \div \boxed{} = \boxed{}$

5 A rectangle has a length of 12 cm and a width of 5 cm.

5 cm

12 cm

CHALLENGE

6 rectangles are used to make a longer rectangle.

?

Use the 6 times-table to work out the length of the shape.

I wonder if I could multiply by 6.

The length of the new shape is ☐ cm.

Reflect

Draw or write your own story involving multiplication or division by 6. Ask a partner to find the solution to it.

Date: _____

6 times-table and division facts

1 Fill in the missing numbers.

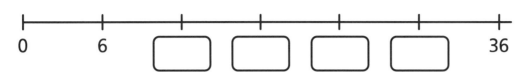

0   6   [ ]   [ ]   [ ]   [ ]   36

2 Which 6 times-table facts do these pictures show?

a)

[ ] × [ ] = [ ]

b)

[ ] × [ ] = [ ]

c)

[ ] × [ ] = [ ]

132

3 Find the solutions to these calculations.

a) $3 \times 6 = \boxed{}$ f) $0 = 6 \times \boxed{}$ k) $12 \div 6 = \boxed{}$

b) $1 \times 6 = \boxed{}$ g) $\boxed{} \times 6 = 24$ l) $30 \div 6 = \boxed{}$

c) $6 \times 6 = \boxed{}$ h) $9 \times 6 = \boxed{}$ m) $42 \div 6 = \boxed{}$

d) $12 \times 6 = \boxed{}$ i) $6 \div 6 = \boxed{}$ n) $60 \div 6 = \boxed{}$

e) $\boxed{} = 6 \times 10$ j) $24 \div 6 = \boxed{}$ o) $\boxed{} \div 11 = 6$

4 Fill in the missing numbers.

a)

| 6 | 12 | 18 | | | | 42 | |

b)

| 60 | | | | 36 | | | |

5 $12 \times 6 = 72$

Use this to work out 13×6.

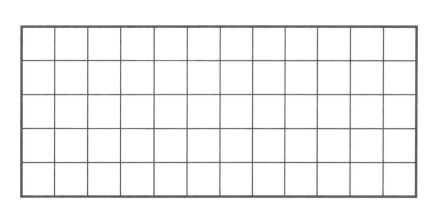

$13 \times 6 = \boxed{}$

6 Complete each calculation using <, > or =

a) $2 \times 6 \bigcirc 10$ d) $18 \div 6 \bigcirc 24 \div 6$

b) $36 \div 6 \bigcirc 30$ e) $9 \times 6 \bigcirc 6 \times 9$

c) $5 \times 6 \bigcirc 7 \times 6$ f) $15 \times 6 \bigcirc 6 \times 12$

133

7 How can you use the answer to 8 × 5 to work out 8 × 6?

CHALLENGE

_____

_____

_____

_____

_____

_____

_____

Reflect

How fast can you complete the 6 times-table?

0 × 6 = ☐	1 × 6 = ☐	2 × 6 = ☐	3 × 6 = ☐
4 × 6 = ☐	5 × 6 = ☐	6 × 6 = ☐	7 × 6 = ☐
8 × 6 = ☐	9 × 6 = ☐	10 × 6 = ☐	11 × 6 = ☐
12 × 6 = ☐		Time taken: _____	

Circle the answers you knew without having to work them out.

Multiply and divide by 9

↓ Textbook 4A p184

1 Complete the number line.

0   9   18   27

2 a) How many hearts are there in total?

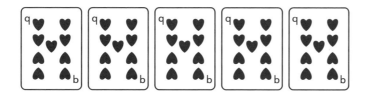

□ × □ = □   There are □ hearts.

b) How many spades are there in total?

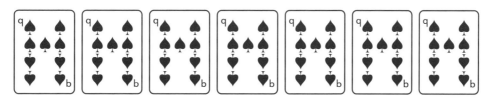

□ × □ = □   There are □ spades.

3 Work out 18 ÷ 9.

18 ÷ 9 = □

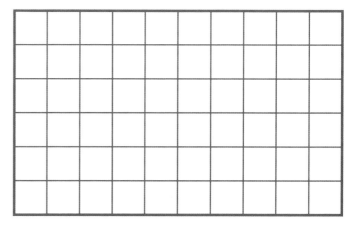

4 Work out 27 ÷ 9.

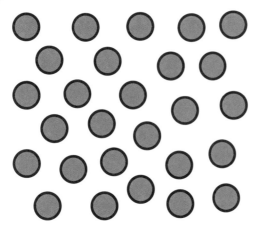
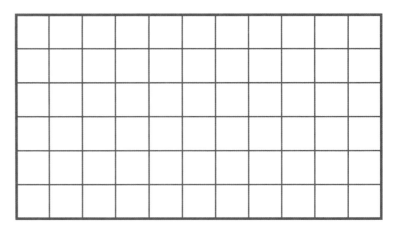

27 ÷ 9 = ☐

5 Mr Lopez's class are going on a school trip.

The cost for the trip is £9 each.

How many children handed in money today?

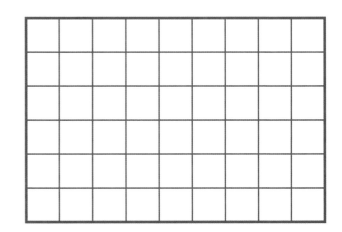

Mr Lopez

Today I have collected £72.

6 Complete the calculations.

a) 2 × 10 = ☐   2 × 9 = ☐

b) 6 × 10 = ☐   6 × 9 = ☐

c) 4 × 10 = ☐   4 × 9 = ☐

d) 8 × 10 = ☐   8 × 9 = ☐

7 Rowan makes the following towers of cubes.

She now puts the cubes into towers of 9.

How many towers can she make?

Rowan can make ☐ towers of 9 cubes.

Reflect

The answer to the problem is £45 ÷ 9 = £5.

What could the problem be? Write or draw your own word or picture problem to match the division.

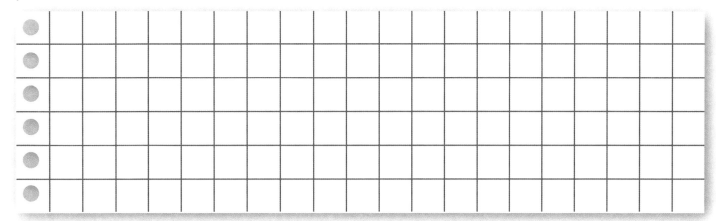

Date: _____

9 times-table and division facts

1 Complete the calculations using the 9 times-table.

a)

$\boxed{} \times 9 = \boxed{}$ $\boxed{} \div 9 = \boxed{}$

b)

$\boxed{} \times 9 = \boxed{}$ $\boxed{} \div 9 = \boxed{}$

c)

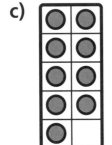 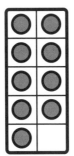 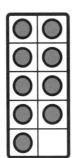 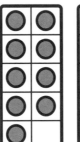 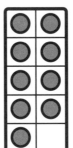 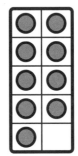 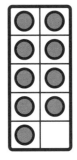

$\boxed{} \times 9 = \boxed{}$ $\boxed{} \div 9 = \boxed{}$

2 Complete the number line.

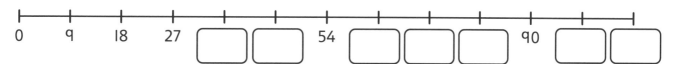

0   9   18   27   ☐ ☐   54   ☐ ☐ ☐   90   ☐ ☐

3 **a)** Complete the array to show 6 rows of 9.

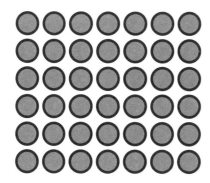

b) Complete the four facts.

6 × 9 = ☐

☐ × ☐ = ☐

☐ ÷ ☐ = ☐

☐ ÷ ☐ = ☐

4 Solve these calculations.

a) 7 × 9 = ☐

b) 0 × 9 = ☐

c) 9 × 9 = ☐

d) ☐ = 9 × 5

e) ☐ = 12 × 9

f) 18 = 2 × ☐

g) ☐ × 9 = 27

h) 9 × ☐ = 9

i) 54 ÷ 9 = ☐

j) 36 ÷ 9 = ☐

k) ☐ ÷ 9 = 11

l) ☐ ÷ 9 = 10

139

5 In pairs, take turns to roll two dice.

Multiply the total score by 9 and record your answers.

How many can you get right in one minute?

Reflect

Write four facts to go with each triangle.

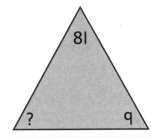 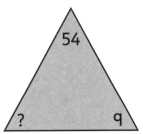 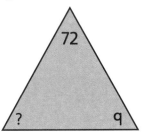 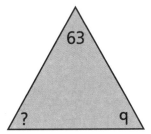

The 3, 6 and 9 times-tables

→ Textbook 4A p192

1 **a)** Count in multiples of 3.

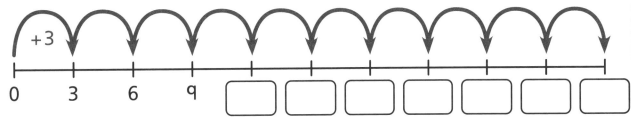

b) Count in multiples of 6.

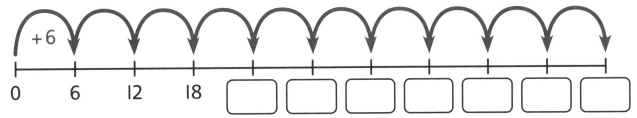

c) Count in multiples of 9.

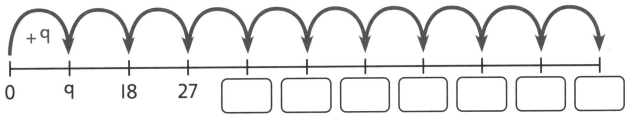

2 Place the numbers in the sorting circles.

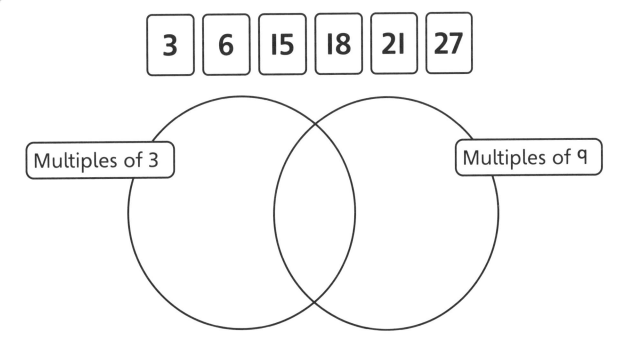

3 Write three numbers in each section of the sorting circles.

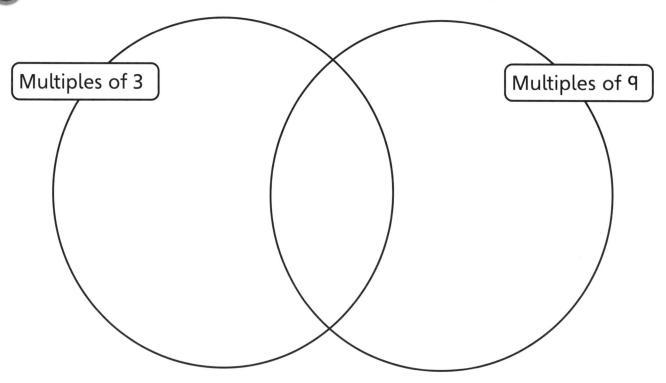

Multiples of 3

Multiples of 9

4 Tick to show if each statement is true.

Statement	True	False
All multiples of 9 are multiples of 3	☐	☐
All multiples of 3 are multiples of 9	☐	☐
All multiples of 3 are even	☐	☐
Some multiples of 6 are odd	☐	☐

5 Complete the number sentences.

CHALLENGE

a) 4×3 = ⬚ $\times 6$

8×3 = ⬚ $\times 6$

10×3 = ⬚ $\times 6$

b) 3×3 = ⬚ $\times 9$

6×3 = ⬚ $\times 9$

9×3 = ⬚ $\times 9$

c) $15 \div 3$ = ⬚ $\div 6$

$21 \div 3$ = ⬚ $\div 6$

$30 \div 3$ = ⬚ $\div 6$

d) $36 \div 9$ = ⬚ $\div 6$

$45 \div 9$ = ⬚ $\div 6$

$63 \div 9$ = ⬚ $\div 6$

Reflect

Write three facts from the 3, 6 and 9 times-tables that you find tricky.

Discuss with a partner how you will learn them.

_____

_____

_____

_____

_____

_____

_____

Date: _____

Multiply and divide by 7

 a) How many cars are parked in the car park?

$$\boxed{} \times \boxed{} = \boxed{}$$

There are $\boxed{}$ cars.

b) How many cubes are there in total?

$$\boxed{} \times \boxed{} = \boxed{}$$

There are $\boxed{}$ cubes.

c) There are 7 biscuits in a packet.

Circle 49 biscuits.

144

2 Complete the number track.

0	7	14		28						

3 Draw lines to match up the correct number of days to the correct number of weeks.

6 weeks	9 weeks	7 weeks	11 weeks

49 days   63 days   77 days   42 days

4 8 ten frames each have 7 counters on them.

How many counters are there in total? ☐   × 8

5 79 counters are put into rows of 7.

a) How many complete rows of counters are formed? ☐

b) How many counters are left over? ☐

6 Alex buys these items.

£7   £7   £7

The total cost of the items is £35.

How much does a bag of popcorn cost?

CHALLENGE

Reflect

Write a story problem for 5 × 7.

7 times-table and division facts

1 Complete the number line.

0   7   14   [ ] [ ] [ ] [ ] [ ] [ ] [ ]   70   [ ]   84

2 Which facts from the 7 times-table do the pictures show?

a)

[ ] × [ ] = [ ]

[ ] × [ ] = [ ]

[ ] ÷ [ ] = [ ]

[ ] ÷ [ ] = [ ]

b)

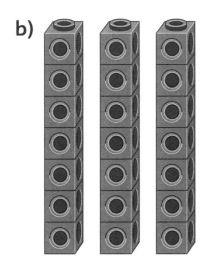

[ ] × [ ] = [ ]

[ ] × [ ] = [ ]

[ ] ÷ [ ] = [ ]

[ ] ÷ [ ] = [ ]

147

3 Work out the answers.

a) $4 \times 7 = \boxed{}$

b) $2 \times 7 = \boxed{}$

c) $7 \times 5 = \boxed{}$

d) $\boxed{} = 10 \times 7$

e) $7 \times 0 = \boxed{}$

f) $\boxed{} = 11 \times 7$

g) $\boxed{} \times 7 = 42$

h) $56 \div \boxed{} = 7$

i) $77 \div 7 = \boxed{}$

j) $7 \div 7 = \boxed{}$

k) $28 \div 7 = \boxed{}$

l) $\boxed{} = 63 \div 7$

m) $\boxed{} \div 7 = 3$

n) $\boxed{} \div 7 = 12$

4 a) Alex used these cubes to work out 8×7.

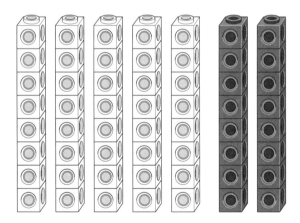

Alex's method:

First, I did $8 \times 5 = \boxed{}$.

Then, I did $8 \times 2 = \boxed{}$.

Finally, I added the numbers together: $\boxed{} + \boxed{} = \boxed{}$.

The answer to $8 \times 7 = \boxed{}$.

b) How can you use 8×7 to work out 9×7?

_____

_____

5 Complete the multiplication wheel.

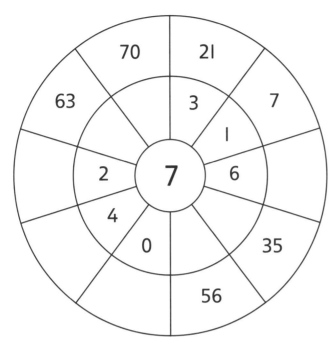

6 I am thinking of 7 times-table facts.

The answer is odd. What fact could I be thinking of?

CHALLENGE

_____

_____

_____

_____

Reflect

Play a game with a partner.

Count up and down in 7s.

Take it in turns to say the number.

Date: _____

11 and 12 times-tables and division facts

1 **a)** Count in multiples of 11.

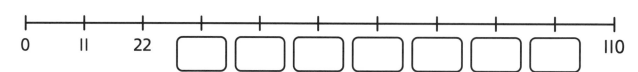

b) Count in multiples of 12.

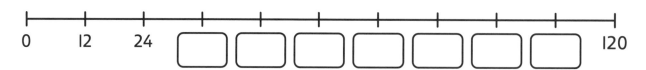

2 Which 11 or 12 times-table facts do the pictures show?

a)

$\boxed{} \times \boxed{} = \boxed{}$ dots

b)

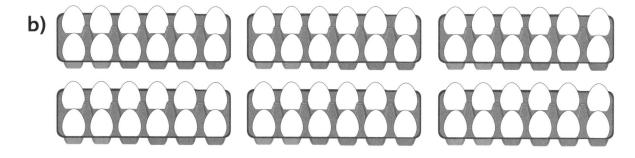

$\boxed{} \times \boxed{} = \boxed{}$ eggs

c)

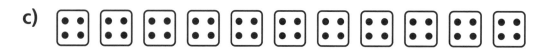

$\boxed{} \times \boxed{} = \boxed{}$ dots

3 Complete the multiplication wheels.

a)

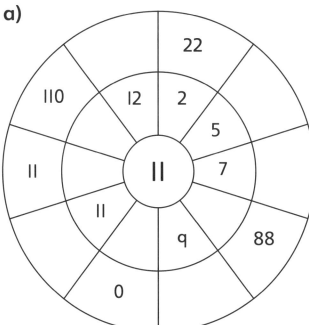

b)

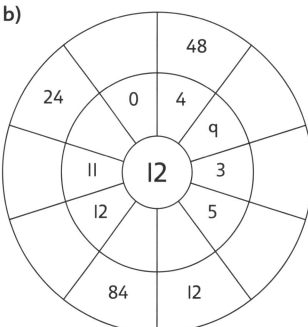

4 Fill in the missing numbers.

a)

22	33				77			

b)

	36		60		84		

c)

132						60

d)

132						66

5 Complete the number sentences.

CHALLENGE

a) $6 \times 12 = \boxed{}$

$\boxed{} \div 12 = 6$

b) $88 \div 11 = \boxed{}$

$88 \div \boxed{} = 11$

c) $\boxed{} = 36 \div 12$

$36 = 12 \times \boxed{}$

d) $132 \div 12 = \boxed{}$

$11 \times \boxed{} = 132$

Reflect

You now know all of the times-tables.
Complete the grid to show off the facts you know.

×	7					11		6		1		
10												
					110			88				
						11						
4											48	
				25								
	42	18	12		60							
								16				
12									12			
7							63					
								24				
9											36	
									8			

Date: _____

Multiply by I and 0

I How many muffins are on each group of plates?

Draw lines to match each picture to the correct multiplication sentence.

a)

$2 \times 3 = \boxed{}$

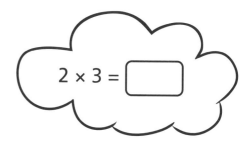

b)

$I \times 4 = \boxed{}$

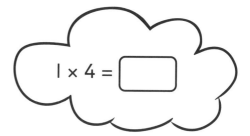

c)

$5 \times I = \boxed{}$

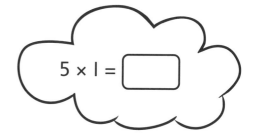

d)

$2 \times 0 = \boxed{}$

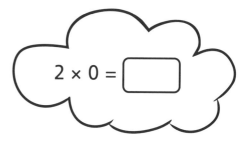

e)

$4 \times 0 = \boxed{}$

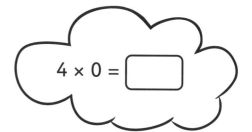

2 Here are 4 trays. Each tray contains the same amount of equipment.

a) How many counters are there in total?

⬚ × ⬚ = ⬚   There are ⬚ counters in total.

b) How many pencils are there in total?

⬚ × ⬚ = ⬚   There are ⬚ pencils in total.

c) How many cubes are there in total?

⬚ × ⬚ = ⬚   There are ⬚ cubes in total.

3 Circle the multiplications that have an answer of 0.

| 3 × 0 | 0 × 10 | 15 × 0 | 6 × 1 |

| 1 × 5 | 3 × 8 | 0 × 5 | 1 × 0 |

What is the same about all of the calculations you have circled?

_____

_____

_____

_____

4 Fill in the missing numbers to make the calculations correct.

a) $7 \times 0 = \boxed{}$

c) $\boxed{} \times 1 = 15$

b) $1 \times 9 = \boxed{}$

d) $\boxed{} = 127 \times 0$

5 Kate has a function machine.

CHALLENGE

Kate puts the number 5 into the function machine.

What number does Kate get out? $\boxed{}$

IN

| ×2 | ×3 | ×4 | ×1 | ×0 |

OUT

Reflect

$\boxed{} \times 0 = \boxed{}$ $\boxed{} \times 1 = \boxed{}$

Look at the two calculations above.

What can you say about the numbers that go in each of the boxes?

_____

_____

_____

Date: _____

Divide by I and itself

 a) There are 6 sweets. They are shared equally between I person.

How many sweets does the person receive?

⬜ ÷ ⬜ = ⬜

b) There are 6 sweets. They are shared equally between 6 people.

How many sweets does each person receive?

⬜ ÷ ⬜ = ⬜

2 What mistake has Amelia made?

4 ÷ 4 = 0

Amelia

_____

_____

_____

3 Circle the calculations that have an answer of 1.

| $8 \div 8$ | | $8 \div 1$ | | $5 \div 5$ | | $16 \div 16$ |

| $20 \div 2$ | | $7 \div 7$ | | $2 \div 1$ | | $150 \div 150$ |

4 **a)** Find the solutions to these calculations.

$3 \div 1 = \boxed{}$ $4 \div 1 = \boxed{}$ $5 \div 1 = \boxed{}$

$10 \div 1 = \boxed{}$ $14 \div 1 = \boxed{}$ $20 \div 1 = \boxed{}$

Complete the following sentence.

When you divide a number by 1 _____

_____

b) Find the solutions to these calculations.

$3 \div 3 = \boxed{}$ $4 \div 4 = \boxed{}$ $5 \div 5 = \boxed{}$

$10 \div 10 = \boxed{}$ $14 \div 14 = \boxed{}$ $20 \div 20 = \boxed{}$

Complete the following sentence.

When you divide a number by itself _____

_____

_____

5 Fill in the missing numbers to make the calculations correct.

a) $11 \div 1 = \boxed{}$ **d)** $9 \div \boxed{} = 9$ **g)** $\boxed{} \div 1 = 0$

b) $11 \div 11 = \boxed{}$ **e)** $12 \div \boxed{} = 1$ **h)** $8 \div \boxed{} = 7 \div 7$

c) $\boxed{} = 25 \div 25$ **f)** $\boxed{} \div 1 = 70$

157

6 $\square \div 1 > \pentagon \div 1$

CHALLENGE

The square and the pentagon represent numbers.

Which statement is true? Tick the correct one.

☐ The square is equal to the pentagon.

☐ The square is greater than the pentagon.

☐ The pentagon is greater than the square.

Explain your answer.

_____

_____

Reflect

$\boxed{} \div \boxed{} = 1$ $\boxed{} \div 1 = \boxed{}$

Look at the two calculations above.

What can you say about the numbers that go in each of the boxes?

- _____
- _____
- _____

Multiply three numbers

↓ Textbook 4A p216

1 What multiplication can you see in each diagram?

a)

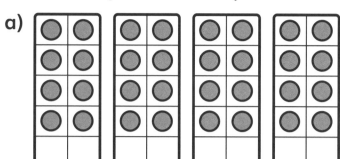

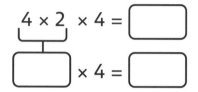

$4 × 2 × 4 = \boxed{}$

$\boxed{} × 4 = \boxed{}$

b)

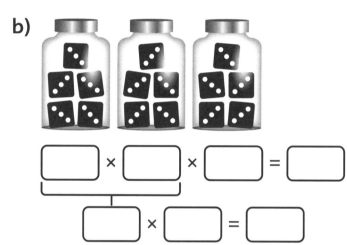

$\boxed{} × \boxed{} × \boxed{} = \boxed{}$

$\boxed{} × \boxed{} = \boxed{}$

2 Jill buys two identical boxes of chocolates.

They contain 24 chocolates in total.

Draw a diagram to represent what the boxes could look like.

3 Aki is working out the answer to 2 × 7 × 9.

He multiplied 7 by 9 first and then multiplied by 2.

Why do you think Aki did this?

_____

_____

_____

4 There are 11 plates with 5 cakes on each plate.

All the cakes are the same.

How many candles are there in total?

[ ] × [ ] × [ ] = [ ]

There are [ ] candles in total.

5 Work out the multiplications.

a) 2 × 4 × 6 = [ ]

b) [ ] = 8 × 5 × 2

c) 4 × 5 × 5 = [ ]

d) 5 × 7 × 3 = [ ]

e) [ ] = 9 × 2 × 4

f) 9 × 2 × 8 = [ ]

6 Fill in the missing numbers.

a) 4 × [ ] × 2 = 32

b) 2 × 7 × [ ] = 70

c) [ ] × 8 × 5 = 80

d) 54 = [ ] × 9 × 2

e) 7 × 0 × [ ] = [ ]

f) 36 = 6 × [ ] × 6

7 Work out the multiplication and then explain to a partner how you did it. Did you use the same method as your partner?

$4 \times 5 \times 7 \times 6 \times 0 \times 3 \times 2 \times 1 = \boxed{}$

_____

_____

8 Write a number from 1 to 9 into each empty box. How many different solutions can you find?

CHALLENGE

$\boxed{} \times \boxed{} \times \boxed{} = 60$

Reflect

How many ways can you work out $2 \times 8 \times 5$?

Which method is the most efficient?

_____

_____

_____

_____

Date: _____

End of unit check

My journal

↑ Textbook 4A p220

1 Jamilla buys some presents for her friends:

- a small present costs £3
- a medium present costs £6
- a large present costs £9.

Jamilla spends £45 in total on presents.

How many of each size of present does she buy?

How many answers can you find?

_____

_____

_____

_____

_____

_____

2 Sort these problems into two types of calculation. Write down the reasons behind your sorting. Then work out the answers.

A: A book costs £6. How much do 7 books cost?	**C**: A board game costs £9. How many board games can I buy with £90?
B: A bag containing 48 sweets is shared equally between 6 children. How many sweets does each child receive?	**D**: The mass of a bag of apples is 18 kg. What is the mass of 9 bags of apples?

I put the problems into these groups: _____

The reason I sorted in this way is _____

_____

_____

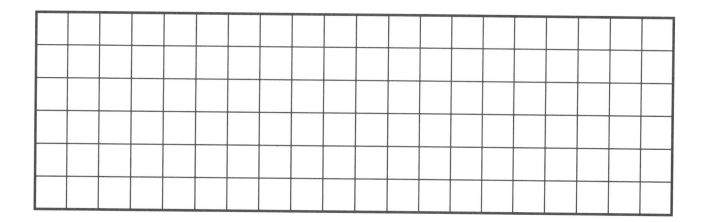

Power check

How do you feel about your work in this unit?   ?

Power puzzle

How fast can you complete each of these multiplication grids?

1 Time to complete:

____ minutes and

____ seconds

×	5	8	4	12	6	9	2	10	11	3	7	1
2												
9												
8												
12												
5												
6												
7												
3												
11												
1												
4												
10												

2 Time to complete:

____ minutes and

____ seconds

Design your own grid for a partner to complete. How many boxes do you need to give them before they can complete all the others?

×		7		4		11		5	10			
4						4						12
						10						
									20	24		
						1						
8	16											
						6	66					
								60				
3							18					
												21
11				88								
9			81									
		35										

164

My power points

Colour in the ☆ to show what you have learnt.

Colour in the ☺ if you feel happy about what you have learnt.

Unit 1

I can …

☆ ☺ Represent 4-digit numbers

☆ ☺ Partition 4-digit numbers

☆ ☺ Find 1,000 more or less

☆ ☺ Use number lines

Unit 2

I can …

☆ ☺ Compare and order numbers to 10,000

☆ ☺ Round numbers to the nearest 1,000

☆ ☺ Estimate on a number line

Unit 3

I can …

☆ ☺ Add and subtract 1s, 10s, 100s and 1,000s

☆ ☺ Add two 4-digit numbers using the column method

☆ ☺ Subtract two 4-digit numbers using the column method

☆ ☺ Find and use equivalent difference and other mental methods

☆ ☺ Estimate answers to additions and subtractions

☆ ☺ Check strategies

☆ ☺ Solve addition and subtraction problems

☆ ☺ Exchange across two columns

Unit 4

I can …

☆ ☺ Find the area of shapes

☆ ☺ Measure area using squares

☆ ☺ Make shapes

☆ ☺ Compare area

Unit 5

I can …

☆ ☺ Multiply and divide by 0 and 1

☆ ☺ Say my 3, 6, 7, 9, 11 and 12 times-tables

☆ ☺ Understand related multiplication and division facts

☆ ☺ Solve multiplication and division word problems

☆ ☺ Multiply three numbers

Keep up the good work!

Squared paper

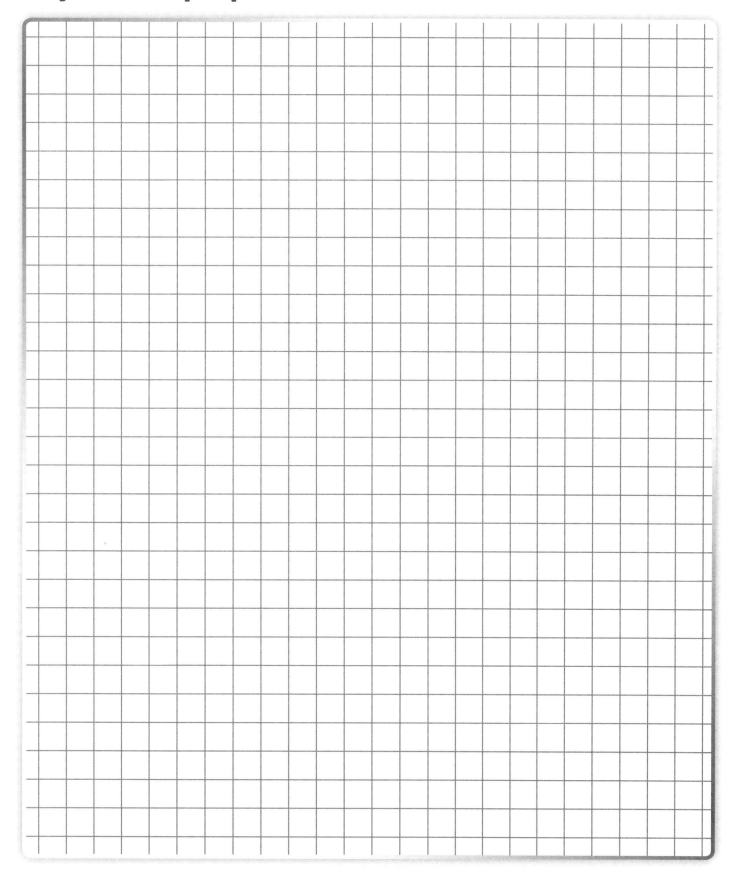

Published by Pearson Education Limited, 80 Strand, London, WC2R 0RL.

www.pearsonschools.co.uk

Text © Pearson Education Limited 2017, 2022
Edited by Pearson and Florence Production Ltd
First edition edited by Pearson, Little Grey Cells Publishing Services and Haremi Ltd
Designed and typeset by Pearson and Florence Production Ltd
First edition designed and typeset by Kamae Design
Original illustrations © Pearson Education Limited 2018, 2022
Illustrated by Laura Arias, John Batten, Paul Moran and Nadene Naude at Beehive Illustration;
and Florence Production Ltd and Kamae Design
Cover design by Pearson Education Ltd
Front and back cover illustrations by Diego Diaz and Nadene Naude at Beehive Illustration.
Series editor: Tony Staneff; Lead author: Josh Lury
Authors (first edition): Tony Staneff, Josh Lury, Neil Jarrett, Stephen Monaghan, Beth Smith
and Paul Wrangles
Consultants (first edition): Professor Liu Jian and Professor Zhang Dan

The rights of Tony Staneff and Josh Lury to be identified as authors of this work have been
asserted by them in accordance with the Copyright, Designs and Patents Act 1988.

First published 2018
This edition first published 2022

26 25 24 23
10 9 8 7 6 5 4 3 2

British Library Cataloguing in Publication Data
A catalogue record for this book is available from the British Library

ISBN 978 1 292 419 459

Printed in the UK by Bell & Bain Ltd, Glasgow

For Power Maths online resources, go to:
www.activelearnprimary.co.uk

Note from the publisher
Pearson has robust editorial processes, including answer and fact checks, to ensure the accuracy of
the content in this publication, and every effort is made to ensure this publication is free of errors.
We are, however, only human, and occasionally errors do occur. Pearson is not liable for any
misunderstandings that arise as a result of errors in this publication, but it is our priority to ensure
that the content is accurate. If you spot an error, please do contact us at resourcescorrections@
pearson.com so we can make sure it is corrected.